Geoff Tibballs has worked as  now a full-time writer and ed eating, drinking and avoiding with his wife. He is the autho including *The Mammoth Book of Jokes* and *Crazy Sh*t Old People Say*.

Also available:

Crap Kitchen
Boiled gannet, calf-brain custard and other 'acquired tastes'
Geoff Tibballs

The Good, the Bad and the Wurst
The 100 craziest moments from the Eurovision Song Contest
Geoff Tibballs

How to Talk Teen
From Asshat to Zup, the Totes Awesome Dictionary
of Teenage Slang
Mark Leigh

The Ludicrous Laws of Old London
Nigel Cawthorne

THE WORLD'S

100

WEIRDEST MUSEUMS

GEOFF TIBBALLS

From the Moist Towelette Museum in Michigan to the Museum of Broken Relationships in Zagreb

ROBINSON

ROBINSON

First published in Great Britain in 2016 by Robinson

Copyright © Geoff Tibballs 2016

13 5 7 9 10 8 6 4 2

A CIP catalogue record for this book
is available from the British Library.

ISBN: 978-1-47213-695-4

Typeset in Great Britain by Hewer Text UK Ltd, Edinburgh
Printed and bound in Great Britain by CPI Group (UK) Ltd, Croydon CR0 4YY

Papers used by Robinson are from well-managed forests
and other responsible sources

MIX
Paper from
responsible sources
FSC
www.fsc.org   FSC® C104740

Robinson
An imprint of
Little, Brown Book Group
Carmelite House
50 Victoria Embankment
London EC4Y 0DZ

An Hachette UK Company
www.hachette.co.uk

www.littlebrown.co.uk

CONTENTS

AFRICA

ASIA

AUSTRALASIA

SOUTH AMERICA

NORTH AMERICA

INTRODUCTION

When we think of the world's great museums, we tend to think of the Louvre, the Guggenheim or the Victoria and Albert. We do not immediately think of the Dog Collar Museum, the Kansas Barbed Wire Museum, the Museum of Broken Relationships, Barney Smith's Toilet Seat Art Museum or the Baked Bean Museum of Excellence. Yet scattered across the globe are museums dedicated to every conceivable subject, from bananas to bagpipes, lawnmowers to leprechauns, torture to tapeworms, mustard to moist towelettes, and pencils to penises. Many are serious collections housed in grand buildings, others are located in tiny premises and open to visitors by appointment only, often the result of one person's crazy lifetime obsession.

So what are the world's 100 weirdest museums? Well, in addition to those listed above, they encompass such delights as The Museum of Witchcraft in Cornwall, a museum in Kentucky that houses 800 ventriloquists' dolls, an underwater museum in Mexico, a museum in a telephone box in Wales, a New York museum located in an old elevator, the Museum of Bad Art in Massachusetts, the Paris Sewer Museum, the French Fry Museum in Bruges, the Cement Museum in Spain, the Umbrella Cover Museum in Maine, the Salt and Pepper Shaker Museum in Tennessee, San Francisco's Antique Vibrator Museum, and the Kunstkamera in St Petersburg, home to Peter the Great's collection of oddities including deformed foetuses and the decapitated head of a love rival preserved in alcohol. After all, what holiday is complete until you have seen a 300-year-old decapitated human head in a jar?

Museums play a vital role in safeguarding our heritage, preserving items – no matter how obscure – that might otherwise be lost for ever. Alas, in these times of economic strife, a number of niche establishments across the world have been forced to close, including Ross-on-Wye's Button Museum, the Paperweight Museum in Devon, California's Moose Museum, and the Celebrity Lingerie Hall of Fame in Hollywood, which displayed underwear worn by movie stars but, despite the presence of one of Madonna's bras, was evidently not supported enough. It hit the headlines in 1992 when, during rioting in Los Angeles, looters ran off with Ava Gardner's bloomers. It can only be hoped that a new establishment will one day emerge to fill what is so clearly a gap in the market and allow the public to be able to gaze once more on such treasures as the actual boxer shorts worn by Tom Hanks in *Forrest Gump*.

The entries here are listed geographically, and each one includes address, contact and admission details, although it should also be noted that many museums will be closed on major holidays such as Christmas and New Year. So if you are planning a visit on a holiday date, it is probably advisable to check in advance. That way, the next time you are in Berlin there will be no excuse for missing out on a visit to the Currywurst Museum, the world's leading museum dedicated to sausages in spicy ketchup.

BRITAIN AND IRELAND

ENGLAND

CUCKOOLAND MUSEUM, TABLEY, CHESHIRE

If the sound of one cuckoo clock is enough to drive you crazy, try being in a place that has more than 700! The Cuckooland Museum houses the collection of brothers Roman and Maz Piekarski, whose love affair with cuckoo clocks began at the age of fifteen, when they trained as clock-makers in Manchester. For more than forty years, the noted horologists and clock restorers have made it their mission in life to acquire the finest cuckoo clocks manufactured in Germany's Black Forest, where the very first model was made back in the seventeenth century. The story goes that a local clock-maker was so captivated by the sound of the church bells informing villagers what time it was that he decided to replicate the idea using a wooden clock and a cuckoo chime.

The museum opened in 1990 and the brothers conduct the tours personally, providing a wealth of background information on each clock. One of the rarest items is a cuckoo and echo clock that perfectly emulates the whistles and bellows the bird makes in the wild. There are believed to be only six of these clocks in the world. Several of the timepieces have a life-sized automaton cuckoo perched on top of the case, while new for 2015 was a small selection of Art Nouveau-style cuckoo clocks. In addition to cuckoos, there are clocks with quails, trumpeters and even one with monks playing bells. All that is missing is a clock where Bill Oddie pops out on the hour.

If you think the brothers lead an idyllic life among so many pieces of ornate craftsmanship, spare a thought for them twice a year at the start and end of British Summer Time. It takes a total of over fourteen hours to put all 700 clocks back or forward. That's dedication.

ADDRESS:	The Old School House, Chester Road, Tabley, Knutsford, Cheshire, WA16 0HL
TEL:	01565 633039 or 07946 511661 (mobile)
EMAIL:	cuckoolanduk@btinternet.com
WEBSITE:	www.cuckoolanduk.net
OPEN:	By appointment.
ADMISSION:	£5. Check prices when booking.

MUSEUM OF WITCHCRAFT AND MAGIC, BOSCASTLE, CORNWALL

Cecil Williamson first developed a fascination for witchcraft in 1916 when, on a boyhood visit to his uncle, who was a Devon vicar, he saw a woman publicly beaten and accused of bewitching cattle. He befriended the woman, and his belief in the occult was strengthened five years later while at Malvern College. Subjected to sustained bullying, Williamson received help from another woman, who lived in the school grounds and claimed to be a witch. She taught him how to cast a spell, and shortly afterwards his chief tormentor broke a leg in a skiing accident and the bullying stopped.

Williamson began collecting witchcraft-related artefacts and in 1947 tried to open a museum in Stratford-upon-Avon, but met with fierce local opposition. Instead he bought an old mill on the Isle of Man where, four years later, he opened his collection to the public as the Folklore Centre of Superstition and Witchcraft, with his friend Gerald Gardner as its resident witch. After the two men fell out (imagine the curses they could have put on one another), Williamson moved the museum to Windsor, but royal officials were apparently none too happy with the idea of having a witchcraft collection on their doorstep and suggested he go elsewhere. So he relocated to the tranquil Cotswold village of Bourton-on-the-Water, where he received death threats, graffiti was painted on walls, dead cats were hung from trees and the museum was fire-bombed. Williamson took the hint, and in 1961 established his museum in the Cornish village of Boscastle, where it remains to this day, attracting more than 35,000 visitors annually.

There are over 2,000 exhibits on display, including human skulls, torture devices, magic charms, Satanic artefacts, a witch's phallic tusk, a history of witch trials, voodoo rituals, and a particularly fetching poppet – a doll that was used as a curse to resolve an unwanted pregnancy. The doll has real pubic hair sewn between its legs and a dagger embedded in its abdomen. Nice.

Williamson died in 1999 (three years after selling the museum at midnight on Halloween), but just when the locals had finally begun to relax and accept that they would not wake up one morning to a plague of locusts or a hail of serpents, on 16 August 2004 Boscastle was hit by a terrible flood of Biblical proportions. Surely it was just a coincidence. Miraculously, the museum and its contents survived largely intact, although fire crews entering the building received a nasty shock when they found its resident waxwork witch Joan lying in the mud.

ADDRESS: The Harbour, Boscastle, Cornwall, PL35 0HD

TEL: 01840 250111

EMAIL: museumwitchcraft@aol.com

WEBSITE: www.museumofwitchcraft.com

OPEN: April–October, Monday–Saturday, 10.30 a.m.–5.30 p.m.; Sunday, 11.30 a.m.–5.30 p.m.

ADMISSION: £5 adults, £4 children and seniors.

CUMBERLAND PENCIL MUSEUM, KESWICK, CUMBRIA

Although not an obvious choice for an adventure day out, the Cumberland Pencil Museum is still enough of a draw to bring in 80,000 visitors a year from all over the world. It does exactly what it says on the tin. There are no white-knuckle rides, no exotic animals: just a lot of pencils. The wildest that kids get to behave here is doing a spot of colouring.

The nearest the museum gets to the 'Wow!' factor is the item that was once the world's longest coloured pencil. Created in 2001, it measures a whopping 26 feet in length. Perhaps it appeals to the British sense of eccentricity because it is utterly – although not literally – pointless. Of greater interest to many is a First World War spy pencil given to Allied servicemen flying on secret missions over Germany. Such pencils contained a rolled-up map of Germany and a compass where the eraser tip should have been. Apparently the Germans never discovered the true purpose of this crafty device. There is also a video on how pencils are made and the complete and utter history of pencil making from the reign of Elizabeth I to the present day. At the end there is a quiz for children to see how much they have learned from the experience. At least there should be something for them to write down their answers with.

The first pencil factory opened in Keswick in 1832, the forerunner of the famous Derwent Pencil Company, and the museum was created in 1981. It has maintained a steady stream of visitors ever since, not only because of what lies under its roof but also, maybe more importantly, because of the roof itself – a major consideration, given typical Lake District weather, when planning a day out.

ADDRESS:	Southey Works, Main Street, Keswick, Cumbria, CA12 5NG
TEL:	017687 73626
WEBSITE:	www.pencilmuseum.co.uk
OPEN:	Daily, 9.30 a.m.–5 p.m.
ADMISSION:	£4.50 adults, £4 students, £3.50 children.

VACUUM CLEANER MUSEUM, HEANOR, DERBYSHIRE

Whereas most boys in the 1980s loved to play with Lego or Transformers, James Brown's favourite toy was his mother's vacuum cleaner. At the age of four, he would help out around the house with her Electrolux 345 Automatic. 'We had a home help, but she didn't get to do much vacuuming,' he remembers. 'My mum probably thought I'd grow out of it, but once I got my hands on our Electrolux I knew I never wanted to let go.' This James Brown became excited when papa's vacuum cleaner got a brand new bag.

When he was eight James actually started collecting vacuum cleaners. 'I spotted a red Goblin 800 lying on a rubbish dump. I took it home, wiped all the muck off it, plugged it in, and it worked. That was one of the most fantastic moments of my life.' In the same way that other parents would ration sweets, his family stipulated that he was not allowed more than six vacuum cleaners at a time, but he used to sneak them into the house and store them in the loft, and by the time he had reached his teens he had around fifty models. From the age of eleven he even started repairing them. 'Teachers used to bring their old vacuum cleaners to school and I used to fix them.'

James estimates that he has spent well over £60,000 on his collection, including splashing out £2,000 on an old gold-plated Kirby model (the Rolls-Royce of vacuum cleaners) from the United States. He can tell the make of a cleaner just by its sound, from the soothing whirr of the Art Deco Electrolux XXX (one of the first machines to feature an on-board tool rack) to the satisfying burble of the 1936 Singer R1 upright with its double-speed roller and variable nozzle. Few are blessed with such a talent.

In 2010, with the help of a grant from the Prince's Trust, James opened Britain's first vacuum cleaner museum, but only has room to display a selection of his record-breaking 300-plus models in his Derbyshire sales and repair shop, Mr Vacuum Cleaner. Also, for security reasons, some of his more valuable cleaners are stored elsewhere. Even so, he is able to exhibit dozens of classic and vintage models dating back to 1919 – a century of automated suction. Cumbersome silver machines from the 1940s stand alongside the sleeker plastic specimens of the 1970s – uprights, cylinders, Dirt Devils, Henry Hoovers, he loves them all . . . within reason. You will almost certainly be able to find your mother's old vacuum cleaner here somewhere, which has resulted in surprisingly large visitor numbers. So if you think the idea of a vacuum cleaner museum sucks, think again.

'All I've ever wanted is to work with vacuum cleaners,' adds James. 'I love the look, the feel, the sound of them. You can't really explain it to people who don't have the same enthusiasm. It's like some people love vintage cars or clocks. For me it's vacuum cleaners. I suppose I'm the ultimate clean freak.'

ADDRESS: 23 Market Street, Heanor, Derbyshire, DE75 7NR

TEL: 01773 712777

EMAIL: mrvacuumcleaner@hotmail.co.uk

WEBSITE: www.mrvacuumcleaner.co.uk

OPEN: Monday, Tuesday, Thursday, Friday, 9.30 a.m.–4 p.m.; Saturday, 9.30 a.m.–1 p.m. Closed Wednesday, Sunday. Call in advance to check.

ADMISSION: Free

BAROMETER WORLD MUSEUM, OKEHAMPTON, DEVON

Museums are always sensible places to visit on rainy days, and nowhere is better at confirming that your weather forecast is correct than Barometer World, the planet's only barometer museum. Established in 1979 by barometer expert Philip Collins, author of numerous books on the subject, it currently comprises a shop, a repair workshop and a museum. Until 2005, it housed the impressive Banfield Family Collection of 350 barometers, but although these have been sold on, there are still enough weather instruments on display to bring a small ray of sunshine to a cloudy day.

The star attraction is a complete working replica of a barometer that is operated by live leeches. The splendidly named Tempest Prognosticator or Leech Barometer or even Atmospheric Electromagnetic Telegraph (so good they named it thrice) was first demonstrated at London's Great Exhibition of 1851. Designed in the style of Indian temple architecture, this gloriously ornate instrument was invented by the aptly named Dr Merryweather, who, according to a contemporary account,

> had observed that during the period before the onset of a severe storm freshwater leeches tended to become particularly agitated. The learned Doctor decided to harness the physical energy of these surprisingly hysterical aquatic bloodsuckers to operate an early warning system. On the circular base of his apparatus he installed glass jars, in each of which a leech was imprisoned and attached to a fine chain that led up to a miniature belfry – from whence the tinkling tocsin would be sounded on the approach of a tempest.

The more leeches that rang the bell, the more likely it was that a storm was brewing. Dr Merryweather called these twelve leeches a 'jury'. It took Barometer World almost three years to reproduce this gold-plated exhibit of Victorian eccentricity, arguably the most bizarre weather forecaster in history, with the possible exception of Ian McCaskill.

The permanent exhibition shows a wide range of weather predictors, including conventional mercury and aneroid barometers, curious antique instruments and natural devices involving frogs and sharks, but not Michael Fish. Each device has its own story, which the well-informed staff will happily recount. Many visitors are so enchanted that they are unable to resist placing an order for a barometer of their own, but with prices rising to several thousand pounds for antique items, you may find it cheaper just to look out of the window.

ADDRESS: Quicksilver Barn, Merton, Okehampton, Devon, EX20 3DS

TEL: 01805 603443

EMAIL: barometers@barometerworld.co.uk

WEBSITE: www.barometerworld.co.uk

OPEN: By appointment.

ADMISSION: £2.50 adults, £1 children.

GNOME RESERVE, PUTFORD, DEVON

Back in 1978 a garden gnome appeared to artist Ann Atkin in a dream. Most people might have seen it as a sign to increase their medication, but Ann saw it as a sign to start making and collecting gnomes, and currently she has over 2,000 of them on display at a gnome reserve in her four-acre woodland garden in Devon, earning her a place in *Guinness World Records*. 'Gnomes are just magical little creatures,' she enthuses. 'They take you away from any cares or worries that are going on in your life, and put a smile on your face.'

Gnomes began their career as garden ornaments during the early 1800s in the German town of Gräfenroda, which is renowned for its ceramics. Sir Charles Isham introduced them to Britain in the late 1860s, arranging them between rocks on his Northamptonshire estate. Rather like grey squirrels, they soon colonised large areas of the country, their preferred habitat being suburban gardens of people with little taste. Isham was a keen spiritualist who believed that the gnomes were representations of real people. Ann Atkin might stop short of that (although three of them lined up could easily pass for a ZZ Top tribute band), but she does ensure that her gnomes are properly cared for, and in winter they are all washed and repainted by hand to make sure they look their best for the following season's crowds.

So that her gnomes don't feel threatened or embarrassed, all visitors are asked to wear a hat, which is provided free of charge. Those wishing to be photographed with the gnomes can also borrow free fishing rods so they blend in. While some of the gnomes appear happy just sitting on toadstools, others can be seen riding motorbikes, flying helicopters or enjoying picnics. A few intrepid gnomes have even created their own space exploration programme, GNASA. The oldest gnome in the reserve, Siegfried, was sculpted by Ann herself in 1979.

In addition to the gnomes that roam free in the grounds, Ann has opened a small museum exhibiting her collection of over seventy antique gnomes.

To those who think garden gnomes are a bit, well, naff, she replies defiantly: 'Fashions come and fashions go, but gnomes go on for ever.'

ADDRESS:	The Gnome Reserve, West Putford, near Bradworthy, North Devon, EX22 7XE
TEL:	01409 241435
EMAIL:	info@gnomereserve.co.uk
WEBSITE:	www.gnomereserve.co.uk
OPEN:	Daily, 21 March–31 October, 10 a.m.–5 p.m.
ADMISSION:	(to reserve, museum and gardens) £3.75 adults, £3.25 children 3–16 years.

HOUSE OF MARBLES, BOVEY TRACEY, DEVON

We tend to think of marbles as a quintessentially British pastime. It has apparently been played since the sixteenth century in the West Sussex village of Tinsley Green, which for over eighty years has been the venue of the keenly contested World Marbles Championship. Yet marbles date back to the civilisations of ancient Egypt and Rome (Roman murals depict children playing marbles), although in those days they were invariably made of stone or clay. The glass marbles that we know and love came about only because glass-makers in fifteenth-century Germany decided to use up left-over bits of glass to make marbles for their children, and to give their wives something to slip over on while tidying up the house. At this stage they weren't made commercially: it was not until 1915 that the mass production of glass marbles began – and even then it was nowhere near West Sussex but in Akron, Ohio.

Set in an historic pottery, the Glass and Marble Museum at the House of Marbles is home to an impressive collection of antique marbles, and tells the story of how marbles have been produced over the centuries. A separate Games Museum features bagatelles from the early seventeenth century and a collection of old board games that used marbles. Some of the marbles on show are real collectors' items, worth in excess of £600 each, so it might be worth looking down the back of the sofa just in case.

The museum boasts half a dozen marble runs, including 'Snooki', which is said to be the largest marble run in the UK, and possibly even the world. Grown men have been known to be glued to it (not literally) for up to an hour, staring in wonderment at its intricate workings. Visitors can also tour the pottery, watch demonstrations of glassblowing, learn about the 4,000-year history of glassmaking and sit outside in the courtyard garden, where the centrepiece is a giant floating marble. There is also a play area for young children featuring skittles, chess and, of course, marbles.

In this hi-tech age, marbles are no longer as commonplace in the school playground as they once were, having gone the same way as cigarette cards, gobstoppers and the nit nurse, but this place may still appeal to your inner child. Just don't be surprised if, when you suggest a visit, the rest of the family think you've lost your marbles.

ADDRESS:	Pottery Road, Bovey Tracey, Devon, TQ13 9DS
TEL:	01626 835285
EMAIL:	enquiries@houseofmarbles.com
WEBSITE:	www.houseofmarbles.com
OPEN:	Monday–Saturday, 9 a.m.–5 p.m.; Sunday, 10 a.m.–5 p.m.
ADMISSION:	Free

DOG COLLAR MUSEUM, LEEDS CASTLE, KENT

Leeds Castle in Kent was once the residence of Catherine of Aragon, first wife of Henry VIII. Its other major claim to fame is that it is now home to a museum containing the world's most significant collection of dog collars.

The museum contains around 200 dog collars, mostly collected by Irish historian John Hunt and his wife Gertrude. After he died in 1979, she presented the collars to Leeds Castle in his memory. The neckwear on display spans six centuries of canine chic, charting the dog's changing status from hunting machine to pet. It ranges from thick iron collars with formidable spikes to protect hunting dogs against the bears and wolves that roamed Europe in the sixteenth century, to decorative seventeenth-century Austrian leather collars, often embellished with metalwork and velvet, for pampered pooches. An ornate Italian Renaissance collar, designed to show off the owner's wealth, has an estimated value of £10,000. And to think that today's mutt is lucky to get a strip of tartan nylon . . .

There are also a number of engraved collars – some, in silver, worn by champion dogs; others, in brass, belonging to those further down the barking order. The inscription on one eighteenth-century English brass collar states: 'I am Mr Pratt's Dog, King St, nr Wokingham, Berks. Whose Dog Are You?'

Before your hound gets too excited about enjoying a dream day out, it should be noted that only guide dogs or hearing dogs are allowed into the museum. You'll just have to tell him about it when you get home.

ADDRESS: Leeds Castle, Maidstone, Kent, ME17 1PL
TEL: 01622 765400

EMAIL: enquiries@leeds-castle.co.uk

WEBSITE: www.leeds-castle.com/Attractions/
The+Dog+Collar+Museum

OPEN: Daily, Apr–Sept (10.30 a.m.–6 p.m.), Oct–March
(10.30 a.m.–5 p.m.)

ADMISSION: (included in the general admission to Leeds
Castle) £24 adults, £21 students and seniors,
£16 children 4–15 years.

TEAPOT ISLAND, YALDING, KENT

When Sue Blazye's grandmother gave her a pair of blue teapots in 1983, little did she know it would be the start of an obsession that would lead to a place in *Guinness World Records* and a museum displaying more than 7,000 different teapots. 'Soon family and friends began to give me teapots,' says Sue, 'and before I realised it, I was a teapot collector. We would go around car boot sales and pick up a few more. It's the thrill of the chase – the chance to get one I don't have is exciting and addictive. That's how you get hooked: you find something that's rare and you get it really cheap. You think, "I will carry on doing this."' As the collection outgrew her house in Sidcup, in 2003 she and husband Keith opened Teapot Island, a home, café and permanent teapot exhibition alongside the River Medway in the picturesque village of Yalding.

'I like the cleverness of the novelty teapots best,' adds Sue, 'the ones where the spout and handle are integrated, almost invisible. We have a series of pots of a man and lady embracing, from the *Kama Sutra*. I love the idea that they've made that into a teapot. I'm not too fussed with antique teapots – they're far too plain and boring.'

Her collection includes teapots in the shape of everyone from Princess Diana to a Dalek, Wallace and Gromit to Darth Vader, and Winston Churchill to Morrissey. There are Beatles teapots, tiny doll's house teapots, and a teapot in the form of a space rocket that is able to make so many cups of tea it could be personally endorsed by Mrs Doyle from *Father Ted*. There is even a teapot of a Buddha sporting an erection and another of a pole dancer, lying on her back with her legs in the air. Fortunately the two pots are kept apart to prevent any risk of her getting up the spout. The exhibits, some of which are hopelessly impractical for the purposes of making and pouring tea, are arranged by subject – sport, transport, celebrities, music, politics, science fiction, animals, Disney characters, and so on.

Sue admits that men are often reluctant visitors to the museum – dragged in by their wives – but leave with new-found admiration for ceramic teapot design. Sadly she lost her Guinness record in 2011 to China's Tang Yu, who claims to have a collection of 30,000 teapots. She is not overly bitter, but doubts that there are 30,000 different teapots in the world – and she should know, because over the years she's spent an estimated quarter of a million pounds on her passion.

Outside stands a ten-foot-tall teapot that was bought on eBay in 2004 and was collected from Germany on a flatbed truck. Giving a new meaning to high tea, it originally came from a theme park in Saudi Arabia. If you want to split hairs, it is probably a coffee pot, but because it is used as a wishing well to raise more than £7,000 for the Kent Air Ambulance, nobody is complaining. The teapot collector had to keep a lid on her emotions when, in 2005, Teapot Island was damaged by fire, and then in 2013 hit by floods. Sadly, Sue was unable to predict either event in the tea leaves.

ADDRESS: Hampstead Lane, Yalding, Maidstone, Kent ME18 6HG

TEL: 01622 814541

WEBSITE: teapotisland.com

OPEN: April–October, Monday–Friday, 10 a.m.–4 p.m.;

Saturday, Sunday and bank holidays, 9 a.m.–5 p.m.; 1 November–18 December, weekends only, 10 a.m.–3.30 p.m.

ADMISSION: £2.50 adults, £1.50 children.

BUBBLE CAR MUSEUM, LANGRICK, LINCOLNSHIRE

The 1950s was the decade in which Europe really took to the open road. Everyone, it seemed, wanted to own a car, but for many it remained an unaffordable luxury, especially when fuel prices rose in the wake of the 1956 Suez crisis. With demand increasing for a cheap form of transport, manufacturers came up with a curious little vehicle called a bubble car, a three-wheeler that took its name from its shape and often qualified for inexpensive taxing and licensing by virtue of being classed as a motorcycle.

A bubble car would set you back about £300 – equivalent to ten weeks' wages at the time. Invariably you climbed in through the front and trundled along at a leisurely pace (although they could do 60 mph with a following wind), generally avoiding steep hills if you had a passenger. For although they were marketed as family vehicles, they were only really practical if you had a small family, both numerically and physically. Overweight uncles and aunts were not encouraged. Alas, the vehicle's bubble was burst in the 1960s by the arrival of the Mini. Suddenly, driving a small car was not only affordable: it was also cool, an accusation that could never be levelled at a bubble car. Over the ensuing years, bubble car production slowed until they became little more than collectors' items, as incongruous on the roads of the 1970s as a horse and cart or a penny farthing.

One person who never fell out of love with them was Paula Cooper, and in 2004 she and husband Mike opened a museum of around fifty microcars – German-built Messerschmitts, with their tandem seating and side-and-roof opening, front-loading Italian Isettas, British Bonds, Berkeleys and Reliants, and any car with an engine capacity of less than 700 cc. 'Microcars were ideal in those days,' says Paula. 'People went from having a scooter, then when they got a partner they added a sidecar, and when it came to having a family, microcars were the obvious next step.'

To reflect their heyday, the museum also contains classic scooters and items of 1950s memorabilia, including toys, clothes, pottery, period shops and a mock-up garage, so that it offers a trip down memory lane as well as a day out for petrolheads. The museum, which was forced to move to larger premises a few years back, hosts an annual rally of bubble car enthusiasts, who converge on Lincolnshire from miles around to swap stories. 'A Messerschmitt owner was telling me how years ago he took his girlfriend out,' remembers Paula, 'and so that they could have a "chat" in the car, he put the front seat outside. But by the time they got to the cigarette stage he was horrified to find the seat had been pinched – and you can't drive a Messerschmitt with no front seat!'

ADDRESS: Clover Farm, Main Road, Langrick, Boston, Lincolnshire, PE22 7AW

TEL: 01205 280037

WEBSITE: www.bubblecarmuseum.co.uk

OPEN: Easter–third week of December, Friday, Saturday, Sunday and bank holidays only, 10 a.m.–5 p.m.

ADMISSION: £3 adults, £1 children.

OLD OPERATING THEATRE AND HERB GARRET, LONDON

Located in the garret of the eighteenth-century St Thomas's Church near London Bridge is the oldest surviving operating theatre in the UK. It was first used in 1822 to serve the female patients of St Thomas's Hospital back in the days before the use of anaesthetics and antiseptic surgery, and at a time when physicians had only recently stopped prescribing the shoving of a patient's head into the carcass of a freshly slaughtered cow as a remedy for tuberculosis, or the passing of a child three times under the belly of a donkey to cure whooping cough. Today the old theatre forms part of a museum displaying the full horrors of medicine before the age of science.

Surgeons had no recourse to anaesthetics until 1846, relying instead on speed (an amputation could be performed in under a minute), and alcohol or opiates to dull the patient's senses. Patient mortality was high, partly because the surgeons of the day were lax in combating infection. They were just as likely to wash their hands after an operation as before, and during surgery wore frock coats that were described as 'stiff and stinking with pus and blood'. Another discomforting sight was the box of sawdust placed beneath the operating table for the express purpose of collecting blood. Health and safety would have had a field day. When St Thomas's Hospital moved in 1862, the operating theatre was partly dismantled, and was only accessible by ladder. Exactly 100 years later, after a century of disuse, it was restored and reopened as a museum, along with the herb garret where opium and various medicinal herbs were once kept in a Victorian version of Superdrug.

Among the primitive instruments on display are devices for bleeding, cupping and trepanning – the quaint surgical procedure whereby a hole was drilled into the patient's skull to treat seizures, fractures and any disorder thought to be connected in some way to the brain. Glass cabinets contain a treasure trove of tools, potions and remedies, while all the theatre furniture is authentic to the period, including the basic wooden operating table and the rows of viewing platforms catering for medical students and inquisitive sightseers. It is easy to imagine a gangrenous leg being removed in record time to the cheers of onlookers.

Just outside the theatre itself, the museum has areas dedicated to the use of animals in medicine, bizarre Victorian contraptions for the hard of hearing, a nice line in amputation saws and a number of human organs pickled in formaldehyde, including a pair of lungs blackened by those infamous London smogs. Look out, too, for a physician's stick, used chiefly for walking but also held across the patient's mouth as a restraint during surgery – as evidenced by the teeth marks on it. Don't have nightmares.

ADDRESS: 9a St Thomas Street, London, SE1 9RY

TEL: 020 7188 2679

WEBSITE: www.thegarret.org.uk

OPEN: Daily, 10.30 a.m.–5 p.m.

ADMISSION: £6.50 adults, £3.50 children.

VIKTOR WYND MUSEUM OF CURIOSITIES, FINE ART AND NATURAL HISTORY, LONDON

There is only one place in the world where you will find a two-headed stuffed lamb, Napoleon's death mask, a hair-ball from a cow's stomach, some McDonald's Happy Meal toys, a tray of 77 bat skulls and a selection of Russell Brand's pubic hairs under the same roof. Artist and collector extraordinaire Viktor Wynd used to display his bizarre tastes at The Little Shop of Horrors in Hackney, until in 2014 he closed the shop and reopened it as a macabre museum.

Explaining the philosophy behind his new venture, he said: 'It's an attack on the IKEA society and cleanliness, modernity and tidiness. I want to live in a Victorian life surrounded by exquisite clutter. It's also an attack on conventional aesthetic values, so we have a Furby, which is seen as completely valueless, sitting next to a rare and valuable skull of an extinct beast, sitting next to Chinese sex toys. I don't recognise a distinction between high and low: it's just if I like it.'

Those of a timid disposition venture at their peril down the spiral staircase into the basement museum of curiosities, as they enter a world of dead babies in bottles, shrunken human heads and mummified mammals. You never quite know what you are going to stumble across next – a tiger skeleton in a cage, the bones of a dodo, the pickled vagina of a Victorian prostitute, a casket containing some of the original darkness that Moses called down upon Earth, an artificial foreskin, a cassette of a John Major speech on the subject of red tape, an assortment of kidney stones, a Victorian mermaid, or a collection of condoms allegedly used by the Rolling Stones. Wynd's love of idiosyncratic art is demonstrated by the doodles of mad women and prisoners, an exhibition of tribal art from New Guinea and the very nails that artist Sebastian Horsley used to crucify himself in the Philippines in 2000.

Wynd denies that his intention is simply to shock. 'If you are going to a curiosity museum, you want to see dead babies. It's what you expect. That isn't what's new; what's new is the idea that dead babies and Furbies are equally attractive.'

There are suspicions that one or two specimens may not be entirely genuine, but this place is such fun that nobody cares. For example, there are no stone tablets from Moses authenticating the darkness, and Russell Brand has apparently yet to verify whether the nest-like mass of pubic hair is actually his (although its sheer volume does him proud). A jar purporting to contain Amy Winehouse's poo is supported solely by a statement from Wynd claiming that he saw her do it. The fact that he also displays a sample of Kylie Minogue's poo suggests that, whereas most fans are happy with an autograph or a selfie, Mr Wynd likes to go the extra mile.

ADDRESS: 11 Mare Street, London, E8 4RP

TEL: 020 7998 3617

EMAIL: info@thelasttuesdaysociety.org

WEBSITE: www.thelasttuesdaysociety.org

OPEN: Wednesday–Sunday, 11 a.m.–10 p.m.

ADMISSION: £4, including cup of tea and biscuit.

BRITISH LAWNMOWER MUSEUM, SOUTHPORT, MERSEYSIDE

If you have ever spent time idly dreaming about the lawnmowers of the rich and famous, a trip to the British Lawnmower Museum could be your ideal day out. For among the 200 years of British lawnmower machinery on display are the very machines that Prince Charles, Nicholas Parsons, Queen guitarist Brian May, Eric Morecambe, Paul O'Grady and Alan Titchmarsh have used to trim their grass, although in HRH's case it is unlikely that he carried out the duties in person. In such elevated circles, the royal lawnmower is a person rather than an object, like the royal egg timer and the royal backscratcher.

The lawnmower was invented by Gloucestershire textile mill worker Edwin Beard Budding in 1830. He designed a machine that was originally designed to trim the nap off the cloth for guardsmen's uniforms, but on a sudden whim he decided that it would also be useful for cutting grass. People thought he was crazy, so he had to test the mower at night when nobody could see him. His cylinder-cutting principal remains the favoured system today, although his device required the services of two men – one to pull, the other to push. Budding seemed unsure of how to market his invention. His advertising declared: 'Gentlemen will find my machine an amusing and a healthy exercise, plus do the work of six men.'

The museum, which opened in 1991, was developed by former lawnmower racing champion Brian Radam. Not one to let the grass grow under his feet, over a period of forty years he has collected and restored more than 600 old lawnmowers that were destined for the scrapyard, of which around 300 (including a Budding original) are on display. Since the early 1970s, lawnmowers have been used for racing as well as cutting grass, achieving speeds of up to 65 mph, and it is a little known fact that the winner of the British Grand Prix for lawnmowers in 1975 and 1976 was none other than Stirling Moss.

An audio track gives visitors a history of lawnmowers from early horse-drawn or steam-powered contraptions – the very thing for when the mowing gets tough – to modern solar-powered models. Extremes include the world's smallest mower, at just two inches in size, and the most expensive, a 1920 Pearson model worth over £30,000. There are also exhibits by manufacturers not readily associated with the garden industry, including Rolls-Royce, Royal Enfield, Dennis and British Leyland, as well as a small domestic ride-on mower from the 1960s, the British Anzani Lawnrider, which had a tendency to tip over on corners. This undoubtedly harmed its sales, because it was not necessarily seen as a desirable attribute while mowing the lawn for the rider to be dumped in the herbaceous border.

The collection is packed together in a few rooms and makes for a diverting hour. It was recently ranked number 12 on a list of the 'Top 100 Places to Visit in Southport Before You Die', putting it just below viewing geese, but slightly more popular than watching the tide come in.

ADDRESS: 106–114 Shakespeare Street, Southport, PR8 5AJ

TEL: 01704 501336

EMAIL: info@lawnmowerworld.com

WEBSITE: www.lawnmowerworld.co.uk

OPEN: Monday–Saturday, 9 a.m.–5.30 p.m.

ADMISSION: £3 adults, £1 children.

COLMAN'S MUSTARD SHOP AND MUSEUM, NORWICH, NORFOLK

The city of Norwich has been synonymous with mustard for more than 200 years, ever since Jeremiah Colman started producing the stuff at a nearby water mill. In 1823, with the assistance of his adopted nephew James, he founded J. & J. Colman. By the early twentieth century Colman's employed over 2,000 people, and future crime writer Dorothy L. Sayers (creator of Lord Peter Wimsey) worked on the company's advertising account in her job as a copywriter. Death from a surfeit of mustard would have been an ingenious way for one of her characters to die. Although Colman's was swallowed up by Unilever in 1995, the brand name lingers on, and roads, schools and a university house in Norwich all still bear the Colman name.

To commemorate the 150th anniversary of Colman's, the Mustard Shop was opened in the city in 1973, and since being re-located to the attractive Art Nouveau Royal Arcade, it has been extended to incorporate a small museum chronicling the history of Colman's Mustard. The premises have been designed to repli-cate a Victorian shop, and the historic exhibits include wartime mustard tins and Art Deco mustard pots. Naturally the shop sells all manner of mustard-related items, including mustard choc-olate – definitely an acquired taste.

In 2015, CNN named it as one of the world's leading food museums, which shows that this modest display can cut the mustard on the international stage. Real mustard fanatics might care to seek out the National Mustard Museum in Middleton, Wisconsin, which boasts nearly 6,000 mustards from over seventy countries, but while the American museum may be considerably larger it does have the disadvantage of being nowhere near as accessible from Great Yarmouth.

ADDRESS: 15 The Royal Arcade, Norwich, Norfolk, NR2 1NQ

TEL: 01603 627889

EMAIL: info@mustardshopnorwich.co.uk

WEBSITE: www.mustardshopnorwich.co.uk

OPEN: Monday–Saturday, 10 a.m.–5 p.m.; Sunday (July–Dec only), 11 a.m.–4 p.m.

ADMISSION: Free

BAKELITE MUSEUM, WILLITON, SOMERSET

Patrick Cook can't understand why more people aren't crazy about polyoxybenzylmethylenglycolanhydride. That's easy for him to say, but not everyone can be as passionate about telephones, television sets, cameras, jelly moulds and hairdryers made from one of the earliest plastics, more commonly known as Bakelite.

Although the Victorians had already invented a couple of plastics, it was Leo Baekeland, a Belgian-born chemist working in New York, who in 1907, for want of something better to do, decided to study the reactions of phenol and formaldehyde. When he patented the resultant material, he gave it the brand name Bakelite. As the first synthetic material that could be mass-produced, Bakelite's heat-resistant properties and electrical non-conductivity made it a natural choice for kitchenware products, cigarette holders and pipe stems, because few things are worse for the average pipe smoker than watching his pipe melt before his eyes. Bakelite also proved particularly useful for electric hot-water bottles, which otherwise would have been a terrifying – nay, suicidal – prospect.

Patrick's love of all things Bakelite is illustrated by the thousands of items on display in his museum, which together weigh an estimated thirty tons: Art Deco trendsetters, familiar household items like coffee pots, radios, vacuum cleaners, washing machines and lemon squeezers, and rare, quirky items from tiny spy cameras to a doll whose nipples are radio dials. It is like stepping into an early 1960s home, with clocks, egg cups, salt and pepper shakers, napkin rings and picnic sets in a dazzling array of colours that did so much to brighten up the households of the time after the years of post-war gloom. The rarest item (definitely not something you would find in the average home) is a Bakelite coffin, which, because of its heat resistance, was not a great success at cremations, as a result of which the undertaking profession failed to warm to it. The museum is housed in a seventeenth-century watermill, where the collection is arranged in a manner that could best be described as informal, like an attic waiting to be cleared. With nothing hidden behind glass cases, visitors are allowed to handle the goods and feel the smooth, elegant curves of the Bakelite. Patrick, who says he fell in love with the material after buying a Bakelite radio in 1969 with money saved up from his paper round, even dares to look back at what life must have been like before Bakelite, with a display of Victorian plastics.

In one of those bizarre fashion vogues, Bakelite jewellery has become highly collectible, to the extent that buyers are warned about cheap imitations, or fakelite. Perish the thought that you could be tricked into purchasing cheap plastic tat instead of expensive plastic tat.

ADDRESS: Orchard Mill, Williton, Somerset, TA4 4NS

TEL: 01984 632133

WEBSITE: www.bakelitemuseum.co.uk

OPEN: Easter to end of October. During school term time, Thursday–Sunday, 10.30 a.m.–6 p.m.; school holidays, daily, 10.30 a.m.–6 p.m.

ADMISSION: £5 adults, £4 seniors and students, £2.50 children over 6; children under 6 free.

MUSEUM OF KNOTS AND SAILORS' ROPEWORK, IPSWICH, SUFFOLK

'Rope and knots are my life, and have been since I was a boy,' says Des Pawson. 'I make things in rope, I write about knots, I teach, talk and research knots and ropework. I collect books on knots and practical rope seamanship, old sailors' ropework, and the tools of the rope and canvas working trades. Rope inspires me.' I think we get the picture, Des: you like rope . . . and knots.

If you share Des's passion for all things ropey, a visit to this private museum at the home he has with his wife Liz will prove an illuminating experience. He opened it in 1996, and can claim without fear of contradiction that his is the largest display on the subject in the UK. 'We believe that the world should recognise the art and skill of knots and sailors' ropework,' continues Des. 'Such items have often not been valued or exhibited by museums. For many years we have collected old and recent ropework and rope-working tools. We also have some interesting examples of the ropemaker's art. We hope to encourage greater awareness by creating this setting to properly display our collection.'

He first became fascinated by ropes as a boy when an uncle gave him a book about knots, and has never looked back. 'For some reason they just talked to me,' he says. When synthetic ropes were introduced by the fishing industry in the 1960s, Des set out to preserve the traditional ropes made of horsehair and hemp.

Gathered over a period of sixty years, his extensive list of arte-facts ranges from modern examples of knotwork from over a dozen countries to a 28-inch-circumference piece of anchor cable from HMS *Victory*. He owns tapered skipping ropes and animal halters, knives with ropework handles, rope mats and fenders, and a rope-handled shaving brush, as well as an enviable selection of sailors' sea chest handles. And Des can spin a yarn about each one.

The Pawsons also run a business, Footrope Knots, selling a wide variety of handmade knotted items, including pulls for dinner bells. It could be described as money for new rope.

Des's mission to make us all rope-aware might not seem quite as important as saving the planet or eliminating world poverty, but his unbridled zeal for such a niche topic can only be admired. If you're still in doubt, note that in 1997 he was awarded an MBE for services to ropes and knots. How long will it take to look around the museum? It depends on your level of interest. How long is a piece of string?

ADDRESS: 501 Wherstead Road, Ipswich, Suffolk, IP2 8LL

TEL: 01473 690090

EMAIL: des@despawson.com

WEBSITE: www.despawson.com/the-museum/

OPEN: By appointment.

ADMISSION: Free

JACK HAMPSHIRE PRAM MUSEUM, RUGBY, WARWICKSHIRE

With the advent of lightweight pushchairs and car carry-cots for transporting babies, the traditional large coach-built prams fell into decline. As the wheels fell off the pram-making industry in the 1970s and many leading manufacturers went out of business, Jack Hampshire and his wife Vicky began touring the country in search of neglected vintage carriage prams. He then repaired and restored them for display at the Bettenham Baby Carriage Museum in his fifteenth-century manor house at Bettenham in Kent.

By 1995, Jack, then 81, had acquired 460 baby carriages, the largest collection in the world, among them the very prams once used by the infant Prince Charles, Diana Dors and John Lennon. Rarely have soiled nappies travelled in such style. However, the prams had outgrown their parental home. Jack's children did not share his enthusiasm for them, and so after his death, much of the collection moved to a new home in Warwickshire at a business called the Baby Farm, so called because it sells baby equipment from a farm. The owners stress that they do not farm babies.

The collection spans over 130 years of baby carriages, from Victorian boneshakers, whose suspect suspension would have had most babies throwing their toys out of the pram, to deluxe post-Second World War models worthy of being walked by a society nanny. Tucked away in a barn, the setting may be less salubrious than Bettenham Manor, but there is enough to interest even the casual visitor for an hour – at a push.

ADDRESS:	The Baby Farm, Pailton, Rugby, Warwickshire, CV23 0QH
EMAIL:	Rachel@thebabyfarm.co.uk
WEBSITE:	www.thebabyfarm.co.uk
OPEN:	By appointment (group tours six times a year).
ADMISSION:	Donations welcomed.

FORGE MILL NEEDLE MUSEUM, REDDITCH, WORCESTERSHIRE

Nottingham is forever associated with lace, and Stoke-on-Trent with pottery, but not a lot of people know that Redditch was once the international hub of the needle and fishing hook industry, and produced ninety per cent of the world's needles. In the 1870s, the town turned out 3,500 million needles a year.

Set in a listed building that houses the world's only remaining water scouring mill (although it is only operational on Tuesday afternoons, at weekends and for school or group visits), the Forge Mill Needle Museum, which was opened by the Queen in 1983, uses models, old photographs, artefacts and recreated scenes to tell the story of needle making in Victorian times. It may sound a genteel occupation, but it was sometimes a matter of life and death. Sharpening needles on a grindstone was an extremely dangerous process. Workers were regularly injured and occasionally killed by shattering grindstones or shards of flying metal, and also had to contend with 'pointer's rot', a sinister lung disease caused by the clouds of metal dust. In the mid-nineteenth century, the life expectancy of a Redditch needle pointer was not much over thirty-five years.

The top floor holds an extensive collection of needle-related items, including knitting needles, tiny surgical needles, a six-foot-long needle (apparently the world's largest) and an unrivalled display of old needle cases. Just when you think you'll faint at the sight of yet another needle and wonder at the very point of a needle museum, there is a display of fish hooks to behold. Fortunately anglers are renowned for their high boredom threshold.

To be fair, despite its unpromising subject matter, the needle museum has a lot going for it, and children will love watching the water mill at work. You may leave with a new respect for the humble needle now that you know how much blood, sweat and toil went into its manufacture. A word of warning: admission is free for Redditch residents on Wednesdays. Don't get crushed in the stampede.

ADDRESS:	Needle Mill Lane, Riverside, Redditch, Worcestershire, B98 8HY
TEL:	01527 62509
WEBSITE:	www.forgemill.org.uk
OPEN:	February–March and October–November, Tuesday–Friday, 11 a.m.–4 p.m.; weekends, 1–4 p.m. April–September, Monday–Friday, 11 a.m.–4.30 p.m.; weekends, 11 a.m.–4 p.m.
ADMISSION:	£4.90 adults, £3.80 seniors, £1.65 children.

MILK BOTTLE MUSEUM, MALVERN, WORCESTERSHIRE

There is no disputing that Steve Wheeler has a lotta bottle – over 20,000 in fact, all stored in the private museum he has created in a large warehouse in his back garden. Known to connoisseurs of dairy produce containers as 'the milk bottle man from Worcestershire', he has been collecting milk bottles for more than thirty years, his interest sparked by the chance discovery while out walking in the Brecon Beacons of a discarded bottle from a dairy (Goodwins of Whitchurch, Shropshire) that was closing down. Sensing that it might one day become a collector's item, he set about acquiring more milk bottles from other dairies ... and more ... and more ... and more.

When he reached 150 bottles, he thought things were spiralling out of control, but little did he realise he was only just getting started. He now has milk bottles from all over the world, including examples from Australia, Canada, the United States and Pakistan, the oldest dating back to 1850 – a Grimwade Patent Milk bottle found by a diver in Sydney Harbour, Australia, for which Steve paid the princely sum of £150. Another early item is the UK's first production milk bottle, a plain specimen sent out by Express Dairy around 1880: on the top it says, 'By appointment to Her Majesty the Queen', which would have been Victoria.

Steve's collection is valued at around £100,000 and weighs in the region of 16 tons. Every item is logged on a computer database so that he can access any bottle when he needs it. He picks up most of them from farms, scrapyards, hedges and hillsides, his quest for rare and unusual bottles taking him to every corner of Britain. He also swaps bottles with fellow collectors. As his fame has spread, he has encouraged people to send any unusual bottles to him rather than throw them away. 'Sadly, when people find an old bottle, they tend to just put it in the bin. It's such a shame.' He has several different bottles from the Royal Dairy Farm in Windsor, but his favourite bottle of all is one bearing a picture of pin-up Zoe Newton – the face of the 1950s 'Drinka Pinta Milka Day' advertising campaign.

'I like the designs and the advertising they put on the bottles,' explains Steve. 'They are all completely individual – there's a fascinating story behind each and every one. They're becoming more important in terms of social history, because everyone just gets their milk in plastic or cardboard containers these days. I happen to like glass.'

He is certainly more interested in the glass than the milk. In fact, he doesn't even like milk, describing it as 'baby food', and has not drunk it neat since he was a boy. He welcomes visitors on a regular basis, and estimates that in an average year some fifty enthusiasts, including milkmen and dairy workers, pass through the doors of his museum to study the bottle-lined shelves.

When he first collected milk bottles, his friends treated it as a bit of a joke, but as he has gone on to become an acknowledged expert in the field, they have started to take him more seriously. 'I try to keep it as serious as I can,' he says, 'because it makes it easier to get more bottles. The secret is, if you want to collect something, make sure it's fun, and doesn't cost much.'

ADDRESS: 16 Leigh Sinton Road, Malvern, Worcestershire, WR14 1JW

TEL: 01684 569656

EMAIL: milkbottlepast@hotmail.com

OPEN: By appointment.

ADMISSION: Free

SCOTLAND

MUSEUM OF PIPING, GLASGOW

Public opinion outside Scotland is often sharply divided about bagpipes. Some people say the instrument burns best on a coal fire; others recommend using a wood stove.

Such views will fall on deaf ears at the Museum of Piping (located in Glasgow's National Piping Centre), which proudly displays 300 years of piping heritage. A sculpture of bagpipes found on an ancient slab indicated that the instrument was played in the Middle East as early as 1000 BC, but the first reference to the Scottish Highland bagpipe is at the Battle of Pinkie Cleugh in 1547, when the Scots used the haunting sound of the instrument to torment and terrify the English. They have been doing much the same ever since. Over the centuries, many other civilisations have played the bagpipes, but most have had the decency to allow the practice to die out.

The museum features displays on bagpipe manufacture, as well as historic specimens from lowland Scotland and other parts of the world. But it is the history and culture of the Highland bagpipe that takes centre stage, with pride of place going to the chanter (which is the melody pipe as opposed to the aptly named drone) of seventeenth-century Skye piper Iain Dall MacKay, the oldest surviving piece of bagpipe anywhere in the world. MacKay's grandson had taken the chanter with him to Canada when he emigrated from Scotland in 1805, but the family returned it to MacKay's homeland in 2010 for display at the museum. Among the other artefacts on show is a piping relic that belonged to Robert Burns.

The Museum of Piping may not have anything to do with plumbing but, unless you're a true devotee of the bagpipes, there may be times during your visit when you wish it did. Oh for the joyous sound of hammer on stopcock! A resident piper performs at the museum every Thursday and Friday during the summer. Don't say you haven't been warned.

ADDRESS:	National Piping Centre, 30–34 McPhater Street, Cowcaddens, Glasgow, G4 0HW
TEL:	0141 353 0220
EMAIL:	museum@thepipingcentre.co.uk
WEBSITE:	www.thepipingcentre.co.uk/museum
OPEN:	Monday–Thursday, 9 a.m.–7 p.m.; Friday, 9 a.m.–5 p.m.; Saturday, 9 a.m.-noon; closed Sunday.
ADMISSION:	£4.50 adults, £2.50 senior citizens, children under 16 and students.

WALES

TELEPHONE BOX MUSEUM, CILGERRAN, PEMBROKESHIRE

If you're looking for a museum dedicated to old telephone boxes, you'll be sorely disappointed by this place, because there is only one phone box, and it has no phone. The name is misleading, for the phone box in question is merely the home for a display of local photographs, making it, if nothing else, one of the world's smallest museums. Whereas the walls of other public phone boxes can be a resting place for dubious business cards, this one is decorated with a gallery of innocent black and white photos depicting life in rural Wales in a bygone era.

It was in 2009 that BT launched an 'Adopt a Kiosk' competition, in which local communities were invited to share their innovative ways of preserving their disused iconic red phone boxes. The Cilgerran Language and Heritage Committee suggested turning the phoneless phone box, which had been bought by the village council for £1, into a tiny gallery exhibiting the work of local photographer Tom Mathias, who had lived in a house just fifty yards away. The idea won an award, and the committee was given £1,000 to build its museum, which eventually opened in May 2011, but only after the original phone box had to be replaced when a vehicle slid on black ice and crashed into it. The replacement box was given a fresh coat of paint inside and out and was ring-fenced by a low slate wall, as befits a proper museum.

Born in 1866, Mathias was a farmer and self-taught professional photographer who captured village life in all its forms on camera – from family gatherings and events to workers at the local slate quarries. He died in 1940, and his glass-plate negatives were left to deteriorate in his greenhouse for thirty years until another photographer, James Maxwell Davis, set about taking prints from the surviving negatives. The result of his painstaking endeavours is the Tom Mathias Collection.

The museum in a telephone kiosk is located at a junction just outside the village, and hundreds of tourists drive past it every day without having any idea what it contains. It won't take you long to look around, and you won't need a guide.

ADDRESS: Red Telephone Box, Garnon's Mill Road, Cilgerran, Pembrokeshire, SA43 2PD

TEL: Ironically there is no phone number.

EMAIL: info@cilgerran.info

OPEN: Whenever nobody else is in the phone box.

ADMISSION: Free

If the experience inspires you to seek out a museum with a multitude of telephone kiosks, try the **Avoncroft Museum of Historic Buildings** near Bromsgrove, Worcestershire, which in 1994 acquired the National Telephone Kiosk Collection. It contains thirty-two different public phone boxes, including every type in UK use from 1912 up to the present day. See website (www.avoncroft.org.co.uk) or call 01527 831363 for details.

BAKED BEAN MUSEUM OF EXCELLENCE, PORT TALBOT, WEST GLAMORGAN

Every day for over twenty years, baked bean enthusiast and former computer worker Barry Kirk has painted his face and bald head orange before donning golden cape, green pants and an orange jumpsuit to transform himself into the world's only haricot bean superhero, Captain Beany. In 1986 he had changed his name to Captain Beany by deed poll, after lying in a bath of baked beans for 100 hours for charity. As befitted his new-found status, he insured himself against alien abduction and drove a Beanmobile, in the form of an old Volkswagen Beetle painted with a baked bean design. His motto is 'to baldly go where no man has bean before', and he bravely entered politics as the founder and sole member of the New Millennium Bean Party. At the 2015 general election, the good Captain contested the Aberavon constituency in Wales and received a staggering 1,137 votes, 3.6 per cent of the total vote. In 2007, he climbed Mount Snowdon while carrying a plate of baked beans on toast, and the following year he took his favourite food around the London Marathon course as the original runner bean. When he's not dressed as a baked bean superhero, he earns a living as a Bono impersonator. It is debatable which of his two identities is the more embarrassing.

After the Beanmobile rusted so badly it was towed away by the council, Captain Beany was forced to travel everywhere by bus, prompting strange looks from his fellow passengers, until he bought an ageing Mini Metro with the number plate H57 (as in Heinz57) on eBay. This prompted his next half-baked venture – spending £10,000 to turn his top-floor orange council flat in Port Talbot, South Wales, into the Baked Bean Museum of Excellence, complete with a fart alarm to deter burglars.

'I have scoured the Internet and made hundreds of telephone enquiries,' he announced. 'Nowhere else in the world is there a baked bean museum. Even Heinz, which used to have a showroom in its Pittsburgh factory, does not have one any more. I'm expecting to get a wide range of people in. There are lots of people out there fascinated by baked beans.'

Among the 500-plus items of bean-related paraphernalia in his small private museum are a two-foot-tall baked bean money box, a baked bean clock and a toy model of a 1960s Heinz lorry. He also has a range of bean-shaped mugs, advertising posters, photographs, jigsaws, plates, tea towels, various brands of tinned baked beans, and even a baked bean bed warmer, although after consuming so many beans it would surely be easier just to let nature do the job. Keeping his finger on the pulse, in 2015 he marked his sixtieth birthday by having images of sixty baked beans tattooed on his head. Each tattooed bean was sponsored, and the money raised went to charity. A visit to the museum is indeed a unique experience, and it certainly helps that the curator is full of beans. Just don't stand downwind of him.

ADDRESS:	6 Flint House, Moorland Road, Sandfields Estate, Port Talbot, South Wales, SA12 6JX
TEL:	01639 698954 or 078038 72428 (mobile)
EMAIL:	captainbeany@captainbeany.com
WEBSITE:	www.captainbeany.com
OPEN:	By appointment.
ADMISSION:	Charity donations welcomed.

REPUBLIC OF IRELAND

NATIONAL LEPRECHAUN MUSEUM, DUBLIN

Most museums like to think big; the National Leprechaun Museum thinks small. Dedicated to the little green folk that roam their way through Irish legends, the museum was conceived by Dublin architect Tom O'Rahilly, and opened in 2010 with the aim of giving visitors 'the leprechaun experience'.

To achieve this, a guide begins by explaining precisely what leprechauns are. They are not elves or trolls, but little people, were first 'sighted' back in the eighth century and are uniformly male, which must have made breeding difficult down the years. Giant pandas are sex machines next to leprechauns. Entering via an optical illusion tunnel, which makes you appear smaller to those at the other end, you are then taken on a tour through a series of rooms, including one where all the furniture is three times the normal size to make you feel like one of the little people. These are apparently the correct proportions of human height to leprechaun height. A rain room, protected by umbrellas so that you don't get wet, is followed by the rainbow room, and then another room featuring a tantalising crock of gold floating over a tree stump. There is also the cautionary tale of a man who tried to catch a leprechaun. This may or may not be entirely true.

By day, the tours are full of Irish whimsy, but the night show explores the darker side of Irish mythology, with bawdy yarns not suitable for young children or anyone who believes in fairies.

For those whose only previous experience of a leprechaun is a sweaty middle-aged guy in a baggy green suit nursing his seventh pint of Guinness in an Irish bar on St Patrick's Day and insisting that you're his best friend, the museum will come as welcome light relief, and may help restore your faith in little human nature. As for whether the elusive crock of gold really exists, it obviously doesn't, because you can't buy one in the gift shop.

ADDRESS: Twilfit House, Jervis St., Dublin 1, Ireland

TEL: +353 1 873 3899

EMAIL: rainbow@leprechaunmuseum.ie

WEBSITE: www.leprechaunmuseum.ie

OPEN: Daily, 10 a.m.–6.30 p.m. Night show, Friday and Saturday at 7.30 and 8.30 p.m.

ADMISSION: 12 euros, adults; 10 euros, students and seniors; 8 euros, children 3–11 years; 3 euros, children under 3.

EUROPE

AUSTRIA

CONDOMI MUSEUM, VIENNA

The majority of early condoms were made from either linen or, more alarmingly, sheep intestines, which led Casanova, surely the finest advert imaginable for the product, to complain, 'I do not care to shut myself up in a piece of dead skin to prove that I am perfectly alive.' Renaissance slaughterhouse workers used sausage skin, while for their part the Japanese wore condoms made from tortoiseshell or thin leather, until the development of the vulcanisation of rubber in 1844 transformed the world of contraception.

Located in the cellar of the specialist erotic shop Liebenswert, the Condomi Museum, open since 2009, traces the colourful history of condoms, the first known description of which was published by Italian anatomist Gabrielle Fallopius in 1564. In the early part of the twentieth century, most condoms were imported from Germany, which meant that when the Second World War broke out, British soldiers often prepared for action stations wearing German condoms. There are around 300 exhibits, including novelty condoms from around the world, with items dating back to 1930. These days you can even buy musical condoms, which play tunes such as 'Happy Birthday', although 'Johnny, Remember Me' might be more fitting. Alongside condoms old and new, there is plenty of educational material about safe sex. Thankfully birth control has come a long way since the ancient Egyptians used crocodile dung as a contraceptive.

To cater for both sexes, the museum is also home to Austria's first vibrator exhibition, which displays curious vintage models, some of which look more like corkscrews or bottle openers. According to legend, Cleopatra used bees captured in bamboo sticks to give herself the ultimate buzz. The museum is always on the lookout for vibrators of historical interest, and encourages visitors to hunt through their bottom drawers for any unwanted mechanisms to add to its 'little collection of lustbringers'.

ADDRESS:	Esterhazygasse 26, 1060 Vienna, Austria
TEL:	+43 1 595 5255
WEBSITE:	www.liebens-wert.at/veranstaltungen/ condomi-museum
OPEN:	Monday–Friday, 11 a.m.–7 p.m.; Saturday, 11 a.m.–6 p.m.
ADMISSION:	Free

NONSEUM, HERRNBAUMGARTEN

In 1901, a certain Thomas Ferry of Wilmington, Delaware invented the moustache guard, a curious device that was strapped around the head to prevent gentleman diners getting food on their precious upper-lip hair. Quite apart from the fact that it looked utterly ridiculous, the moustache guard was not exactly an invention that was going to change the course of the world. Priced at $2, and therefore considerably more expensive than a simple napkin, it was an extravagance men decided they could do without. Ferry would have encountered many a kindred spirit at the Nonseum, a museum of nonsense located in Lower Austria, close to the Czech border, which unashamedly showcases over 250 'inventions that we do not need'.

The Nonseum was founded in 1994 by sculptor Fritz Gall and four other local artists, who came up with the idea after organising Austria's first fair of failed inventions. Soon the small village of Herrnbaumgarten was being overrun by 5,000 visitors a year – some from such far-flung lands as China and South Korea – as the museum acquired a cult following among fans of the absurd. Each exhibit has its own peculiar charm, whether it is a pair of keyhole-shaped glasses designed for voyeurs, or a soup plate with a plug, which allows you to drain unwanted food discreetly without the risk of offending your host.

The displays are not to be taken seriously, and the quirky Austrian humour may leave some visitors baffled. For example, 'the world's one and only collection of famous buttonholes' – including the third buttonhole from the top of Napoleon's military vest – is naturally nothing but a row of empty boxes. Another splendid collection features dozens of single socks picked up from all over the world. The tricycle for twins is particularly ingenious – a four-wheeled contraption with the two seats facing in opposite directions, and designed in such a way that the riders would be constantly pedalling against one another, and therefore travelling precisely nowhere. For celebrities intent on privacy, a much cheaper option than designer sunglasses is the anonymity shade, a strip of black card on a stick that can be held up before the eyes. Stylish? Probably. Pointless? Definitely. Look out, too, for the set of half-plates and cups for divorced couples, a pair of rounded scissors for faster haircuts, a safety ski incorporating metal spikes on the base, a deck of transparent playing cards, a lever-operated hat that opens at the top so that the wearer can cool his head, a champagne cork catcher, and a fish fork with an attached mirror so that diners can spot bones.

If you need an antidote to the high culture of Vienna, the Nonseum could just be the answer. The contents may even prove inspirational, meaning that if you're really lucky you could find an automatic nose picker in your next Christmas stocking.

ADDRESS: Friedhofstrasse 2a, 2171 Herrnbaumgarten, Austria

TEL: +43 2555 2737

EMAIL: info@nonseum.at

WEBSITE: www.nonseum.at

OPEN: Palm Sunday–All Saints' Day (1 November), Thursday and Friday, 1–6 p.m.; Saturday and Sunday, 10 a.m.–6 p.m.

ADMISSION: 8 euros, adults; 3.50 euros, children.

AZERBAIJAN

BAKU MUSEUM OF MINIATURE BOOKS, BAKU

If you usually head straight for the large print books at the local library, it might be best to give this place a miss, because some of the books are so tiny that they can only be read with a magnifying glass. Three Japanese books published in 1978 measure just 2 mm square.

Miniature books were particularly popular in the seventeenth and eighteenth centuries, and were designed to be carried around in the pocket by readers on the go in much the same way as commuters today read their Kindle on the way to the office. Just as much care goes into the manufacture of miniature books as their full-sized cousins, and the exhibits here feature intricate bindings in leather, wood, snakeskin and silver.

Established in 2002, the museum is located in the old part of Baku, and features a selection of the 6,000 or so miniature books from sixty-seven countries collected over a thirty-year period by dedicated bibliophile Zarifa Salahova. Fortunately, being miniatures, they don't take up too much shelf space. There are small versions of many Azerbaijani classics, and more than 300 titles by Russian poet Alexander Pushkin, as well as an antique miniature copy of the Koran. It is fair to say that lovers of Soviet literature will probably derive most pleasure from the experience, although those looking for a lighter read are catered for by a miniature version of the celebratory royal wedding tome *Prince William and Catherine*. This is the one where the groom stands 1 foot 11 inches tall.

ADDRESS:	67 Bakı AZ 1000, Azerbaijan
TEL:	+994 12 492 9464
OPEN:	Tuesday, Wednesday, Friday, Saturday, Sunday, 11 a.m.–5 p.m.
ADMISSION:	Free

BELGIUM

CARROT MUSEUM, BERLOTTE

Believed to be the world's only bricks-and-mortar museum dedicated to the humble carrot, this quaint establishment is certainly different. There is no entrance, there are no staff and it is always open. That is because the museum consists of nothing more than a single window in a disused electricity substation in the Belgian village of Berlotte near the German border. Since the building is too small to accommodate visitors, they stand outside and peer through the window at the fascinating carrot displays, moving from one exhibit to the next by turning a handle.

It was founded by members of a local men-only organisation known as the MZV (*Möhren Zucht Verein* or 'Carrot Fan Club'), who can be identified by the prominent carrot statues in their gardens. Another giveaway is that they often wear T-shirts with 'MZV' printed on the front. However, they do not all have red hair. Their window displays are '100 per cent dedicated to carrots' (no other root vegetables are permitted), and take the form of novelty arrangements such as carrot necklaces and carrot characters. If you want to find out about the history and cultivation of the carrot, read a book.

Outside the museum you will find a carrot clock, a carrot weather-vane, a carrot light and a carrot design on the ground in stone. Should you happen to visit around mid-November, the Carrot Club organises an annual festival, the highlight of which is the crowning of the Carrot King.

Since the whole set-up is delightfully eccentric, if you ever find the museum visitor's book, expect to see the name B. Bunny at the top.

ADDRESS: Berlotter Strasse, Eyantten, Raeren, 4731 Belgium

OPEN: Always.

ADMISSION: Free

FRENCH FRY MUSEUM, BRUGES

One of the most inexcusable cultural oversights must be the fact that until recently there was not a single museum anywhere in the world dedicated to French fries. Happily this omission was rectified in 2008 by lamp collector and food lover Eddy Van Belle, who, encouraged by the success of a chocolate museum, Choco-Story, he had opened in Bruges, decided to focus his attention on that other staple ingredient of the Belgian diet, the chip.

The *Frietmuseum* is housed on two floors of one of the oldest buildings in the picturesque city, the fourteenth-century Saaihalle, and charts the history of the potato from its origins as a bitter tuber in Peru over 10,000 years ago to today's favourite junk food. Although chips are known internationally as French fries, the Belgians lay claim to their invention in the late eighteenth century. According to the *Frietmuseum*, Belgians used to catch small fish, fry them and eat them whole, but then during a severe winter the rivers froze, so they cut and fried small fish-shaped potatoes instead. Naturally this is disputed by the French, while other scholars suggest the chip was invented in Spain. The Belgians even have a rational explanation as to why the dish is called 'French fries'. They say that fries were first introduced to US soldiers during the First World War by Belgium's French-speaking Walloons, whom the soldiers erroneously assumed were French, and the name stuck. Although there is no documented evidence to support either of the Belgians' assertions, Van Belle, who runs the museum with son Cedric (a chip off the old block), is suitably unimpressed by all rival claimants, and states that 'therefore it is not only normal, but even absolutely necessary, that the first potato fry museum should be opened in Belgium.' So that's that. The science is settled.

The *Frietmuseum* aims to bring chips to life for younger visitors via its two mascots, Fiona Fry (Stephen was unavailable) and Peter Potato. There are around 400 exhibits, including ancient potato cutters, a collection of chip art, a gallery showing fries in cartoons, an assortment of retro chip fryers, and a short video showing the process of turning a potato into perfect fries. Posters on the fry-coloured walls reveal slices of fascinating potato facts. Did you know that potato juice is meant to be a good cure for indigestion, or that the largest potato ever grown weighed a whopping 8 lb 4 oz? After touring the museum, which takes around forty-five minutes, you can pop down to the basement for a lunch of beer and – what else? – fries.

While there is a danger that your children may subsequently suffer nightmares about Peter Potato being slashed with a sharp knife and thrown into a pan of boiling oil, the museum offers an entertaining insight into a food that we tend to take for granted. Of course, to be a true reflection of Belgian dining, the entire *Frietmuseum* should really be covered in mayonnaise.

ADDRESS: Vlamingstraat 33, 8000 Bruges, Belgium

TEL: +32 50 340150

WEBSITE: www.frietmuseum.be

OPEN: Daily except Christmas and New Year, 10 a.m.– 5 P.M.

ADMISSION: 7 euros, adults; 5 euros, children.

LAUNDRY MUSEUM, SPA

The Belgian town of Spa in the Ardennes is usually associated with the country's epic Formula One grand prix circuit, but since 1993 it has had another claim to fame, as home to a museum chronicling the working and living conditions of Spa washerwomen from ancient times right up to the present day.

If you long for the days of the mangle and washboard, *Le Musée de la Lessive* is your dream destination. It occupies twenty-five small exhibition rooms in which you can learn, among other things, about the history of soap and some of the products used before its invention. The first soap was made by the Babylonians around 2800 BC by mixing fats with salts. In those days it wasn't used for bathing or personal hygiene but for cleaning cooking utensils and treating skin diseases. The ancient Greeks were fastidious bathers, but preferred to clean their bodies with blocks of clay, sand, pumice and ashes, blissfully unaware that the ideal medium was being used on their pots. The ever-inventive Romans sometimes made soap from urine, and it was Roman women who, according to legend, discovered that a mixture of melted animal fat and wood ashes, which had soaked into the clay soil along the Tiber from Mount Sapo where animals were routinely sacrificed, made their wash cleaner and for much less effort. Not just clean but bright, sparkling clean – or *clara, glauca et pura*, as the Roman advertising probably went. Some scholars claim that the word 'soap' derives from Mount Sapo. The museum also has a reconstruction of an old wash house, a fine display of vintage irons and washing powder advertising, and a range of early wooden washing machines, some with a rotating drum design. Even in the nineteenth century, when the favoured method was to agitate the clothes with a wooden dolly, washday was said to be as exhausting as swimming five miles of energetic breaststroke. Think of that the next time you moan about the pile of washing.

The first electric washing machine appeared in 1907, while a luxury Magnet model from 1929 featured attachments for making ice cream and sausages. One wonders how many men later found sausage meat in their shirt sleeves. The launch of the twin tub in 1957, and the arrival of the automatic washing machine in the 1960s, revolutionised washday. There was no longer a place in society for the washboard and mangle. We will remember them.

ADDRESS: Rue Hanster 10, 4900 Spa, Belgium

TEL: +32 87 771418

OPEN: Every Sunday throughout the year, 2–6 p.m. Daily, Easter holidays and July–August, 2–6 p.m.

ADMISSION: 3 euros, adults; 1 euro, children.

CROATIA

MUSEUM OF BROKEN RELATIONSHIPS, ZAGREB

When the four-year relationship between Zagreb-based film producer Olinka Vištica and sculptor Dražen Grubišić came to an end in 2003, the two joked about setting up a museum to house all the leftover personal items. Over time they realised that the idea had serious potential, and began asking their friends to donate objects relating to their own break-ups. The Museum of Broken Relationships (Croatian: *Muzej Prekinutih Veza*) now houses hundreds of artefacts mostly from failed romances, ranging from letters and photographs, wedding dresses and teddy bears to a pair of pink fluffy handcuffs, a nasal spray, a prosthetic leg and an axe.

The collection was first shown to the public in 2006, and then went on a world tour for four years, during which time it was seen by over 200,000 people, before in 2010 it finally found a permanent home in Zagreb. The following year it was named 'Most Innovative Museum' at the European Museum Awards. It now regularly attracts up to 1,000 visitors a week, the best-selling item in the obligatory gift shop being a white rubber entitled 'Bad Memories Eraser'.

Each exhibit is accompanied by a brief description. Some of the stories behind the items are touching and sad; others are just weird. The 'ex-axe' was donated by a woman from Berlin, who used it to hack her cheating female lover's furniture to pieces after first throwing her out of the home they shared. 'Every day I axed one piece of her furniture,' wrote the donor. 'I kept the remains there, as an expression of my inner condition. The more her room filled with chopped-up furniture, the better I felt. Two weeks after she left, she came back for the furniture. It was neatly arranged into small heaps and fragments of wood. She took that trash and left my apartment for good. The axe was promoted to a therapy instrument.'

Every object tells a story. The caption on a suspender belt, purchased in Bosnia in 2003, reflects, 'I never put them on. The relationship might have lasted longer if I had.' 'After four years,' laments a woman given an edible G-string as a love token, 'he turned out to be as cheap and shabby as his presents.' On a similar theme, a wife contributed the outsize fake breasts her husband made her wear during sex. Unsurprisingly, she says, they marked 'our biggest relationship crisis.'

From the male perspective, there is a battered pocket watch that an elderly gentleman had bought for his young lover. 'I thought she liked things that were old and broken,' runs the accompanying text, 'but it turned out she didn't.'

One of the more curious items on display is a garden gnome, injured after being hurled in fury by a Slovenian wife at her husband's car windscreen. Another donor, a war veteran, presented the museum with a prosthetic lower leg after he broke up with his physiotherapist.

And what of the founders? Vištica's nickname in the relationship was 'Bunny', and the symbol of their love was a white, wind-up rabbit. It occupies pride of place in the museum.

The exhibits are rotated from time to time, which means that you can visit more than once and invariably see something new . . . like the handful of amputated dreadlocks submitted by a Norwegian man. 'These are my dreads,' he explains in his note. 'Morbid, I know. But notice the braided ends. I didn't do that. Must have been every week for a year. She even tied them together using matching sewing thread. Our nuptial knots. Ten years old, a cut-off from our lives. They belong in a museum.'

Fortunately Zagreb has the very place.

ADDRESS: Ćirilometodska 2, 10000 Zagreb, Croatia

TEL: +385 1 485 1021

EMAIL: info@brokenships.com

WEBSITE: brokenships.com

OPEN: Daily (except holidays) from 9 a.m.

ADMISSION: 30 HRK (nearly £3)

CZECH REPUBLIC

SEX MACHINES MUSEUM, PRAGUE

When visitors wax lyrical about the romance of Prague, they usually have in mind the Charles Bridge, the Tyn Church or the hilltop castle – and probably not the Sex Machines Museum. That might be an oversight, because if there is one place guaranteed to remain in your thoughts long after all the chocolate box images have started to fade, it is this.

Established in 2002 by Oriano Bizzochi despite objections from some city officials who found its content 'disagreeable', this three-floor museum occupies one of the historic houses close to the Old Town Square. According to the official blurb, it describes itself as 'an exposition of mechanical erotic appliances, the purpose of which is to bring pleasure and allow extraordinary and unusual positions during intercourse.' Some of the 200 or so items on display are helpfully accompanied by flexible mannequins so that you can understand precisely how they are intended to work, which really is invaluable, because many are so mind-bogglingly weird that they would have left Casanova scratching his head in bemusement.

The contraptions include a 'copulation table' with foot braces – designed to facilitate unconventional, even weightless, sex positions – body harnesses, and BDSM masks and domination chairs for the *Fifty Shades of Grey* enthusiast. Other instruments are designed for the 'stimulation of penile, scrotal, anal, vaginal and clitoral tissue', such as devilish finger-spikes, which look more like instruments of torture than pleasure, and a bizarre sex machine with an array of phallic knobs and handles that could have been designed by Willy Wonka in his blue period. There is also a throne chair with a large hole in the seat for intimate admiration of a partner's genitalia. Some of these appliances date back to the sixteenth century, but even older are a pair of shoes worn by prostitutes in ancient Greece, which had the words 'Follow my steps' cunningly engraved on the soles so that they left an imprint on the ground.

In addition to devices for encouraging sex, there are a number of items designed to prevent it, such as chastity belts with clawed teeth, and corsets made from iron of a thickness that might have saved the *Titanic*. A fearsome piece of apparatus from a German women's prison was created to soothe the 'fervent feelings' of the inmates, while an early twentieth-century anti-masturbation kit from France involved placing an electronic ring on the boy's penis. The ring switched on automatically in the event of an erection, causing a bell to ring in his parents' bedroom so that his mother could rush in and give him a stiff lecture.

A small cinema shows some early Spanish pornographic films from the 1920s, and there is also a museum shop where you might find something to tickle your fancy. Entertaining though it is, the Sex Machines Museum is probably not somewhere to take your granny, if only because the last thing you want to hear her say is, 'I used to have one of those.'

ADDRESS: Melantrichova 18, 110 00 Prague, Czech Republic

TEL: +420 227 186 260

WEBSITE: www.sexmachinesmuseum.com

OPEN: Daily, 10 a.m.–11 p.m.

ADMISSION: 250 CZK (about £7)

DENMARK

BOTTLE PETER MUSEUM, AEROSKOBING

Everyone likes to have a hobby, but for Danish sailor Peter Jacobsen (1873–1960) his chosen pastime came dangerously close to an obsession. In the course of his lifetime, he built more than 1,700 ships in bottles, earning him the nickname 'Bottle Peter'. His collection, some of which dates back 100 years, has been exhibited in the former poorhouse of Aeroskobing on the island of Aero since 1943, when the local mayor, seeking a tourist attraction, offered Jacobsen and his British wife a home in exchange for the right to display his little ships to the public. When interest in ships in bottles was at its height in the 1950s, the *Flaske-Peters Samling* (Bottle Peter Museum) attracted more visitors than the National Museum in Copenhagen. In 1956, it even received a visit from King Frederik IX of Denmark, with whom Bottle Peter apparently engaged in jolly banter.

Jacobsen went to sea at the age of sixteen, and was employed on ships for the next twenty years, working his way up to chief steward. Taught by a Finnish sailor how to build ships in bottles, he made his first in 1889 when he was still just sixteen, and his last in 1957 when he was eighty-four. He claimed that he drank the contents of every bottle he used except those which contained milk. Perhaps to prove that he could build miniature ships without feeling the urge to insert them in a bottle, he also built fifty larger model ships, which are exhibited here along with a few tiny vessels in cigar boxes.

The most impressive item in the museum is a giant hand-blown bottle containing sixteen ships and an entire town, including shipyard and harbour. There is also a memorial cross he made for his own grave featuring seven bottle ships, one for each of the seven seas he sailed. One might have expected him to be buried at sea – or even in a glass bottle. Instead he was laid to rest in the local cemetery, but without his memorial cross, which his widow insisted should remain with the rest of his collection.

To reach the museum, you will need to travel on a ship that definitely won't fit in a bottle – the ferry from Svendborg to Aeroskobing.

ADDRESS: Smedegade 22, Aeroskobing, Aero 5970, Denmark

TEL: +45 6252 2951

EMAIL: info@arremus.dk

WEBSITE: www.arremus.dk

OPEN: June–August, daily, 10 a.m.–4 p.m.; April–May, September–October, daily, 11 a.m.–3 p.m.; November–March, Tuesday–Friday, 1–3 p.m., Saturday, 10 a.m.–noon.

ADMISSION: DKK 40 (nearly £4)

FINLAND

BONK CENTRE MUSEUM, UUSIKAUPUNKI

Before you get too excited by the title, this is not a 1970s Finnish sex museum based on *Confessions of a Sauna Cleaner*. It is no less peculiar, however, being a satirical museum exhibiting the worthless products of an entirely fictional multinational corporation. Confused? You will be.

Bonk Business Inc. was created by the Finnish artist and sculptor Alvar Gullichsen in 1988 as an art project aimed at parodying the modern corporate world, its language and its advertising methods. It exploited the fact that nobody in the rest of Europe – let alone the world – really has much idea what Finland does. According to the Bonk blurb, the company was founded in 1893 by Pär Bonk, a member of a local fishing family who, in his own eureka moment, discovered that all manner of inventions could be powered by anchovy oil. Bonk's creations proved so successful across the globe that it apparently employs 13,000 people in 52 countries. It is now the world leader in pioneering Third Millennium technologies such as cosmic therapy, fully dysfunctional machinery and ADS (Advanced Disinformation Systems).

Designed by Gullichsen, Bonk's absurd masterpieces, which have been built with commendable period authenticity and have no use whatsoever, are displayed in the Bonk Centre Museum.

They include the paranormal 'mind reading' cannon, the Raba Hiff Eggstream and various other contraptions that would not look out of place in a Terry Gilliam animation.

The centre is a poker-faced testimony to the oddball Finnish sense of humour. Children need not feel excluded from the joke, as there is a workshop where they can construct their own pointless Bonk machines. They do not receive wages, but the compassionate company points out that 'neither are they charged for swallowed nuts and bolts.' Whether you appreciate the museum or think it is worth eight euros to be bombarded with corporate speak probably depends on your ability to think outside the box. But once you've got all your ducks in a row, you could always run it up the flagpole and see if anyone salutes.

ADDRESS: Siltakatu 2, 23500 Uusikaupunki, Finland

TEL: +358 2 841 8404

EMAIL: bonk@bonkcentre.fi

WEBSITE: www.bonkcentre.fi

OPEN: Late June–early August, daily, 10 a.m.–6 p.m.; early June and late August, Tuesday–Saturday, 11 a.m.–3 p.m.

ADMISSION: 8 euros adults; 5 euros students and seniors; 3 euros children 4–12 years.

FRANCE

CORKSCREW MUSEUM, MÉNERBES

It may seem hard to believe, but the corkscrew was actually invented by an Englishman. Moreover, the English bottled wine before the French did. Of course, the French have made up for it since, to the extent that a corkscrew is now one of the essential items in a French household. Set in the Domaine de la Citadelle wine estate in the Provence-Alpes region, *Le Musée du Tire-Bouchon*, which opened in 1993, contains more than 1,200 corkscrews, some dating back to the seventeenth century.

The design of the corkscrew is thought to be based on the gun worm, a device used by seventeenth-century musketmen to remove unspent charges from the barrel of the weapon. The earliest corkscrews were handmade by blacksmiths or silversmiths and, as such, almost every one was unique. Invariably T-shaped, they were often used for opening bottles of beer, perfume or ink. The first corkscrew patent was granted to Revd Samuel Henshall, an English clergyman, in 1795, and it was with the industrial era that the shape of the glass bottle changed from the 'onion bulb' to the familiar cylindrical form we know today. At the same time, the bottle neck became narrower, and the cork was introduced to ensure a perfect seal. A plug extractor or corkscrew thus became indispensable, and in the nineteenth century corkscrews began to be mass-produced in factories.

Among the museum's exhibits are antique corkscrews made of gold, ivory and silver, many with ornate designs in the form of human figures or animals. There is a set of Louis XVIII corkscrews, a wooden pocket series in the form of a set of keys, plus corkscrews that have been incorporated into a walking stick, a ring, and even a revolver. The care and attention that has gone into making them shows just how much importance is attached to the only thing that comes between the French and their wine. As if looking at hundreds of corkscrews is not excitement enough for one day, the real treat is a trip to the cellars for the opportunity to taste the estate's award-winning wines. Best not to mention that you think wine tastes better out of a box.

ADDRESS: Domaine de la Citadelle, 84560 Ménerbes, France

TEL: +33 4 9072 4158

OPEN: April–October, daily, 10 a.m.–noon, 2–7 p.m.; November–March, daily except Sunday and bank holidays, 9 a.m.–noon, 2–5 p.m.

ADMISSION: 3.50 euros adults; children under 16 free.

MUSEUM OF AUTOMATONS AND ROBOTS, SOUILLAC

Where do old mechanical dolls, animals and puppets go when their toy shop closes down? It would seem they head for Souillac in south-west France, to spend a leisurely retirement at *Le Musée de L'Automate et de La Robotique*, a collection of antique automatons that some visitors – including children – may find somewhat creepy. For this is no ordinary toy store: it is one where nearly all of the inhabitants are alive.

Most of the mechanisms in the museum have been restored to working order, so it can be unnerving to watch a snake charmer suddenly spring into life, and a man laugh so heartily that his sides shake. Among the most impressive routines are the Chinese magician who makes his model disappear by ringing a gong, a 1920s Afro-American jazz band, a Parisian subway scene with geese on the tracks, a girl skipping rope, an animated Charlie Chaplin, and the rabbits that emerge from a bunch of cabbages and eat the leaves. Others hark back to the days of seaside postcard humour – a genre that has inevitably been crushed under the weight of modern political correctness – such as a 1948 scenario showing a plump lady trying to pull her skinny husband from the mouth of a large fish.

The majority of the items were made in the workshops of Roullet Decamps, and the very best of the animated scenes once graced the shop windows of Parisian department stores as an attraction to lure young customers and their parents inside at Christmas. Jean Roullet started out in 1865 as a Paris toolmaker, until one of his customers asked him to build a mechanical toy. Roullet quickly saw the potential, and by 1878 had formed a company to mass-produce top-of-the-range automatons. The company catalogue from that year features all kinds of performing animals – bears, dogs, cats and monkeys, usually playing musical instruments or doing acrobatic routines. If you wanted a toy dancing bear for Christmas, Roullet was your man. His creations were crafted with care. The rabbits were wrapped in real rabbit fur, and his peacocks were decorated with genuine peacock feathers. With the help of a reed and bellows paper, many of these toys were able to reproduce accurately the animal's cry.

Provided they are made of stern stuff, children should find this museum an entertaining diversion for an hour – so long as the clever mechanical exhibits don't give them unrealistic expectations of their pet's abilities. Fido can be taught to sit, stay and fetch, but probably not to play Bach's Fugue in D Minor while simultaneously performing cartwheels.

ADDRESS:	Place de l'Abbaye, 46200 Souillac, France
TEL:	+33 5 6537 0707
EMAIL:	musee.automate@wanadoo.fr
WEBSITE:	www.musee-automate.fr
OPEN:	April, May, June, September, October, daily except Monday, 10 a.m.–noon, 3–6 p.m.; July, August, daily, 10 a.m.–12.30 p.m., 2–6.30 p.m.; January, February, March, November, December, daily except Monday, 2.30–5.30 p.m.
ADMISSION:	7 euros, adults; 5 euros students and concessions; 3 euros children 5–12 years.

MUSEUM OF VAMPIRES AND LEGENDARY CREATURES, LES LILAS

The approach to *Le Musée des Vampires et Monstres de l'Imaginaire* on the outskirts of Paris is suitably sinister. The entrance is via a small courtyard at the back of the building, and leads into an eerie garden mocked up like a cemetery, with plastic bats and genuine human bones hanging from the trees. Finally a heavy black and scarlet door creaks open ominously to reveal a room cluttered with centuries of vampire folklore. This is the home of Jacques Sirgent, one of the world's leading experts on all things vampire-related, so visitors to the small private museum might expect to be greeted by a Christopher Lee lookalike who drinks vials of blood. Fortunately Sirgent is relatively normal, even if his specialist subject is anything but.

His fascination with vampires began at the age of ten, when he bought a poster of the horror movie *Dracula Has Risen From the Grave*. He opened the museum in 2005, and is particularly intrigued by the legend of Erzsébet Báthory, the sixteenth-century 'Blood Countess' of Transylvania, who, in the days before Botox, slaughtered and sucked the blood of some 650 young women in order to improve her complexion. Sirgent is also a respected scholar, responsible for the first complete translation of *Dracula* into French.

The two-hour visits are by prior appointment only, are reasonably priced (they won't bleed you dry), and are conducted in both French and English by Sirgent himself. A natural storyteller, he regales his guests with dark tales of Parisian cemeteries where vampiric rituals were practised, some more recently than you may think. His collection, chiefly acquired online or in flea markets and spread over three rooms, includes a vast number of antique books on vampirism, paintings of vampires, movie posters, the autographs of every famous actor to have played Dracula in a Hollywood movie, Halloween props, an authentic nineteenth-century vampire-killing kit, and even a mummified cat found in Paris's Père Lachaise Cemetery. The city's cemeteries are among his favourite haunts and are another source of his vampire memorabilia, among them a slice of tree trunk chopped down because it was swallowing a grave. On certain Sundays he conducts day-long tours, which take in a visit to the museum and, after a picnic lunch, an enlightening trip to the Père Lachaise Cemetery.

It would almost be disappointing if the museum were not haunted, and so it is a pleasure to report that Sirgent claims to have seen a ghost on at least half a dozen occasions, always sitting in the same orange velvet armchair. He says it is the ghost of his grandfather, who killed himself 'for love' by jumping from a tree in the courtyard outside the museum. Although this place is seriously spooky, one crumb of comfort is that Sirgent only opens up for at least two people. So you never have to venture into his macabre museum alone.

ADDRESS:	14 Rue Jules David, 93260 Les Lilas, France
TEL:	+33 1 4362 8076 or +33 6 2012 2832
EMAIL:	museedesvampires@sfr.fr
WEBSITE:	museedvampiresetmonstresdelimaginaire.com.
OPEN:	By appointment, for groups of 2–30 people. Bookings can be made on the website.
ADMISSION:	8 euros per person for museum only, 16 euros per person for all-day tour.

PARIS SEWER MUSEUM, PARIS

As any visitor to the French capital will tell you, Paris is so proud of its sewers that it allows pedestrians to smell them on every street corner. So it should come as no surprise that it has a museum, *Le Musée des Égouts de Paris*, dedicated to its remarkable sewage system.

No other city in the world boasts a sewage network like Paris, stretching out over 1,300 miles of tunnels. More than 5,000 tons of solid waste are removed from the sewers each year, a weight equivalent to around 1,000 elephants – not that anyone is suggesting that there are elephants living in the Paris sewers. Not any more.

From 1889 until around 1970, no trip to the city was complete without a trip to the Eiffel Tower, Sacré-Coeur, Notre Dame and an insanitary tour of the sewers by cart or boat. Those tours have now been replaced by the museum, which offers an alternative view of Paris, a glimpse of the effluent society. It helpfully details the history of the sewers from their initial development in the late fourteenth century to their restructuring in the nineteenth century by the engineer Eugène Belgrand. Visitors walk along a 500-metre underground (dry) tunnel, and still get to see muck first-hand by strolling across raised walkways with the sewage running below. The museum provides information on the methods of water treatment, depicts scenes of sewage workers in action (or, being France, between strikes), and if all that were not glamorous enough in this most romantic of cities, there is an exhibition of sewer-maintenance equipment past and present. As the museum is actually located among the sewers, you may need to hold your nose from time to time.

Naturally there is a gift shop. Cuddly rat, anyone?

ADDRESS:	Pont de l'Alma, left bank, opposite 93 Quai d'Orsay 75007, 7th Arrondissement, Paris, France
TEL:	+33 1 5368 2781
OPEN:	May–Sept, daily, except Thursday and Friday, 11 a.m.–5 p.m.; October–April, 11 a.m.–4 p.m.
ADMISSION:	4.30 euros adults; 3.50 euros students and children. Holders of the Paris Museum Pass, free.

WALLPAPER MUSEUM, RIXHEIM, ALSACE

In addition to being the inspiration for many a slapstick comedy routine, wallpaper hanging has long been a major contributor to the divorce rate, as tempers sometimes become as frayed as the wallpaper itself. It always seems to tear, fold back on itself at will, coat your face in paste and, when finally in place, leave a huge bubble at the least accessible point. Yet to experts it is a thing of great beauty, and this unique museum proudly boasts over two centuries of wallpaper.

Le Musée de Papier Peint was founded in 1982 by the industrialist Pierre Jaquet, but the manufacture of wallpaper in the city of Rixheim, which is located near the German border, dates back to 1797. There are over 100,000 different designs on display, including vast panoramic images of nineteenth-century Boston, Egypt and the Niagara Falls, all of which were calculated to transform Victorian parlours into exotic settings.

Most of the exhibits are taken from the collection of the local Zuber and Cie factory, whose North American patterns proved so popular that in 1961 Jackie Kennedy used 'Views of America', which depicted scenes of the 1830s, to decorate the diplomats' reception room at the White House. She bought it from a farmhouse in Maryland that was being demolished, Zuber wallpaper being of such high quality that when people move home they often take it with them. That particular panorama consists of 32 panels, each of which was block printed by hand and took weeks to make. Its scenes were created from 223 hand-mixed colours and 1,690 carved pear-wood blocks painstakingly stamped onto the paper one at a time and hung to dry in between each paint layer. A Zuber design is certainly not cheap, but is very much the luxury brand of wallpapers. No doubt Jackie decided against allowing JFK to hang it.

Although wallpaper suffered something of a fall from grace after the 1970s, resulting in the closure of a number of manufacturers, it has recently undergone a renaissance. It could be time to dust down that old pasting table in the back of the garage.

ADDRESS:	La Commanderie, 28 Rue Zuber, 68171 Rixheim, France
TEL:	+33 3 8964 2456
EMAIL:	musee.papier.peint@wanadoo.fr
WEBSITE:	www.museepapierpeint.org
OPEN:	Daily, 10 a.m.–noon, 2–6 p.m., except holidays, and closed Tuesday, November–April. Call in advance for guided tour.
ADMISSION:	8 euros (under 16 free if accompanied). Group rates (over 20 people) 5 euros per adult.

GERMANY

DEUTSCHES CURRYWURST MUSEUM, BERLIN

Perhaps deciding that a museum dedicated to the sausage was simply too random, Germany has come up with one which focuses specifically on hot pork sausage seasoned with tomato ketchup and curry powder – or currywurst, as the snack is known locally. Situated near Checkpoint Charlie in Berlin, unsurprisingly this is the first and only museum in the world about currywurst. Yet it is clearly to Germanic tastes, as it attracts around 350,000 visitors annually.

The museum opened in 2009, sixty years after the invention of the currywurst by Berliner Herta Heuwer in 1949. Back then post-war rationing was still in place in West Berlin, and Heuwer began experimenting with ingredients provided by British soldiers stationed in the city. The museum's founder, Martin Löwer, considers the currywurst to possess 'cult status' in Germany, and reckons that a museum in its honour was the very least it deserved. 'No other national German dish inspires so much history and has so many well-known fans,' he enthuses, backed up by figures that show that 800 million currywursts are consumed by Germans each year, while Berlin alone has 2,000 currywurst stands. As the museum's slogan proclaims: 'Currywurst is more than just a sausage – it is one of life's experiences in Germany.'

An array of interactive exhibits guides visitors along a 'sauce trail' chronicling the history of the dish. The emphasis is on testing the senses, so a spice chamber offers several sniffing stations, while audio speakers relay the sound of currywurst cooking. You can also play at being a wurst-seller by having yourself photographed standing behind the counter of a mocked-up currywurst stall, which is really exciting for anyone who has never stood behind anything before. There are currywurst-themed video games to play, and the chance to watch a 2004 documentary film titled *Best of the Wurst*. The rarely discussed role of the currywurst in popular culture is covered at length – Uwe Timm wrote a 1993 novel on the subject (which controversially claimed that the snack was invented in Hamburg), and German rock musician Herbert Grönemeyer once composed a hit song titled 'Currywurst'. At the end of the visit you can relax on a giant 'sauce sofa' shaped like a squirt of ketchup, or call in at the museum shop, which presents the unmissable opportunity to purchase a cuddly currywurst.

ADDRESS:	Schützenstrasse 70, 10117 Berlin, Germany
TEL:	+49 30 887 18647
EMAIL:	info@currywurstmuseum.com
WEBSITE:	currywurstmuseum.com
OPEN:	Daily, 10 a.m.–6 p.m.
ADMISSION:	11 euros adults; 7 euros children 6–13 years; free children under 6.

GHERKIN MUSEUM, LEHDE

As any cucumber connoisseur will tell you, for more than 150 years the Spreewald, a wetland region in the east of Germany, has been famous for its gherkins. For the local population, the Sorbs, a Slavonic people who have lived there since the sixth century, the gherkin is more than just a way of pimping your burger: it is a way of life. Back in the 1870s, a single Spreewald merchant could expect to sell 48,000 gherkins a week, and today's farmers produce 36,000 tons per year. That's a lot of gherkins. So where better to locate what is claimed to be the world's one and only gherkin museum?

Situated in one of the oldest buildings in the picturesque lagoon village of Lehde, a protected heritage site that until 1929 was only accessible by boat, and still receives its post via yellow punt, *Das Gurkenmuseum* brings alive the story of cucumber cultivation and processing. This private museum of the Starick family is crammed to the brim with gherkin trivia and artefacts, including photographs, equipment and over 100 gherkin recipes. The gherkins are stored in barrels, some of which hold 500 gallons, making them big enough to live in, although it is not recommended. There is also a replica of a traditional Sorbian home, where the entire family slept in one room with the baby in a drawer. At least he or she didn't have to share it with gherkins.

The highlight of the visit is the opportunity to sample some Spreewald gherkins, and if you happen to be there in August you can see the coronation of that year's Gherkin Queen, very much the pickling community's answer to Miss World. A mark of the product's importance to the region is that the annual Spreewald Marathon (a combination of running, cycling, hiking, canoeing and drinking) is started with the words, '*Auf die Gurke, fertig, los!*'

(On the gherkin, set, go!) In the 2003 movie *Good Bye, Lenin*, the only way an ailing mother could be convinced that the old East German ideals were being maintained under unification was for her son to bring her some Spreewald gherkins.

One tip: give this place a miss if you don't like gherkins.

ADDRESS:	An der Dolzke 6, 03222 Lehde, Lübbenau, Germany
TEL:	+49 3542 89990
EMAIL:	info@spreewald-starick.de
WEBSITE:	www.spreewald-starick.de
OPEN:	April–October, 9.30 a.m.–5 p.m., and at other times of the year by appointment.
ADMISSION:	5 euros

MOUSETRAP MUSEUM, NEROTH

In the early nineteenth century, the Eifel region of Germany was an impoverished land plagued with rodents. In the absence of a pied piper, the women residents of the small town of Neroth opted for a less humane approach and, inspired by a local school-teacher, started building their own wire mousetraps. Some of their husbands earned a living as travelling salesmen, and began selling the traps throughout Germany and into what is now Poland and the Czech Republic. The demand for Neroth mouse-traps grew to the point where a thriving cottage industry sprang up, and the town became synonymous with murdering mice. The trap sellers always worked in pairs, and even used their own secret language called Jenisch to communicate with one another. All good things come to an end, however, and handmade traps were eventually replaced by mass production. The last mousetrap workshop in Neroth closed in 1979, although one lady still produces traps as souvenirs for tourists.

Nevertheless, the town coat of arms continues to feature a silver mousetrap, and the intriguing *Mausefallenmuseum*, which opened in 1990 in the old Grade II-listed school, documents the work and life of the mousetrap makers in the setting of a recon-structed workshop, along with dozens of examples of their handiwork.

Every conceivable mechanical means of bringing about the premature demise of a mouse can be found here: simple blocks, basket traps, water traps, sinister rattletraps and elaborate ground catchers. Some devices spared the mouse; others were less forgiv-ing. Of particular interest will be a lethal, baited three-holed contraption called the Irish Trap, even though it was made in Germany. The trap was set by means of a piece of string and a wire noose or choker. The mouse had to gnaw through the string in order to reach the bait, but in doing so it released the choker . . . with unfortunate consequences. A number of the traps on display have been donated to the museum by collectors around the world – yes, people actually collect mousetraps. In 2002, the museum was expanded to include a shop specialising in the sale of Neroth wire products, including, of course, souvenir traps. After all, nothing says 'I love you' quite like a handmade mousetrap.

ADDRESS: Mühlenweg 1, 54570 Neroth, Vulkaneifel, Germany

TEL: +49 65 91 81121

EMAIL: MausefallenmuseumNeroth@web.de

WEBSITE: www.neroth.de/index.php/mausefallenmuseum.
html

OPEN: April–October, Wednesday, 2–6 p.m.; Friday, 3–5
p.m. Small group bookings available in winter
via Marianne Horn-Hunz (Tel: +49 65 91 5822) or
Helga Wallenborn (Tel: +49 65 91 3890).

ADMISSION: 3 euros adults; 1 euro children.

HUNGARY

SZABÓ-SZAMOS MARZIPAN MUSEUM, SZENTENDRE

Visitors to Budapest seeking a day's respite from the city could do a lot worse than take a ninety-minute boat trip along the Danube to the charming market town of Szentendre. It is crammed with arts and crafts shops, and in the very centre is the Szabó-Szamos Marzipan Museum, the only place in the world where you are likely to be greeted by full-sized marzipan sculptures of Michael Jackson and Princess Diana. True, without the aid of a label you might struggle to recognise the figure as Diana (who knew she was Barbra Streisand's twin sister?) but you have to make allowances. It is marzipan, after all.

The museum was founded by Szabo Karoly, Hungary's 'Marzipan King', a man with over sixty-five years of marzipan-making experience, and someone who clearly liked to play with his food. In 2003, the Szamos confectionery family took over its running and added their own artworks. Today it contains pieces old and new, including an eight-foot-high cake that took three months to create, and a remarkable model of the Hungarian Parliament Building in Budapest, as well as other local landmarks and famous Hungarians, all in marzipan. Equally impressive are scenes from Harry Potter, *The Wizard of Oz, Puss in Boots, Snow White and the Seven Dwarfs* and various Hungarian folk tales.

Mickey and Minnie Mouse are there, too, along with Yogi Bear and Boo Boo and the Muppets. You have to say they have made a better job of replicating a cartoon bear than an English princess. Maybe Yogi's social diary was less full, giving him more time to pose for the sculptor.

After watching a real marzipan sculptor at work, you may choose to call in at the adjoining café, where you can consume as much marzipan as you can take – so long as you don't try and eat a slice of Michael Jackson.

ADDRESS:	Dumsta Jenõ utca 12, 2000 Szentendre, Hungary
TEL:	+36 26 311 931
WEBSITE:	www.szamosmarcipan.hu
OPEN:	Daily, 10 a.m.–6 p.m.
ADMISSION:	500 HUF (about £1.20)

ICELAND

ICELANDIC PHALLOLOGICAL MUSEUM, REYKJAVIK

The Icelandic Phallological Museum showcases retired teacher Sigurdur Hjartarson's lovingly assembled collection of over 280 penises from 93 different kinds of mammal, ranging from the 67-inch front tip of a blue whale's penis (the entire thing would extend an eye-watering 16 feet) to the tiny 2-mm-long member of a hamster, which can only be seen with a magnifying glass, or by another hamster.

Hjartarson's interest in male genitalia was first aroused in childhood when he was presented with a cattle whip made from a bull's penis. When he later became head teacher at a school in Akranes, some of his colleagues used to work at a local whaling station, and began bringing him whale penises as a joke. This only enabled Hjartarson to see the potential for collecting penises from other types of Icelandic mammal, and before long had acquired seals', walruses', goats', and a rogue polar bear's. Once asked why the fascination with collecting mammal penises, he replied: 'Somebody had to do it.'

Hjartarson, who on special occasions has been known to wear a bow tie made from the penis skin of a sperm whale, opened his collection as a museum in 1997, and it now attracts 11,000 visitors a year – sixty per cent of them women – although staff at the local tourist office are said to blush with embarrassment if asked for directions and information. Judging by the photographs posted online, visitors are particularly impressed by the elephant penis, which hangs down proudly from a wall-mounted plaque. Inevitably the museum guest book includes comments such as, 'I've never seen so many penises – and I went to boarding school!'

In 2011, the museum obtained its first human penis (generously donated by a ninety-five-year-old Icelander and former womaniser, Pall Arason, on his death), but its detachment did not go according to plan and it was reduced to a small, shrivelled heap barely worthy of exhibition. So Hjartarson says he is still searching for 'a younger and a bigger and better one.' To this end, the museum has obtained 'legally certified gift tokens' for four human penises.

Although Hjatarson's daughter has shied away from too much active involvement in the business ever since she had to tell a group of slaughterhouse workers on their lunch break that she was collecting a frozen goat penis for her father, his son, Hjörtur Gisli Sigurdsson, has now taken over the day-to-day running of affairs, thus becoming the world's only second- generation curator of a penis museum.

The museum also exhibits phallic art, including a lampshade made from a bull's scrotum and moulds of the penises of every member of the 2008 Icelandic handball team. There are even the supposed penises of elves and trolls, but since Icelandic folklore depicts these creatures as invisible, these exhibits amount to empty jars. You just have to close your eyes and use your imagination. Your wife will show you how it's done.

ADDRESS: Laugavegi 116, 105 Reykjavik, Iceland

TEL: +354 561 6663

WEBSITE: www.phallus.is

OPEN: Daily, 1 May–30 September, 10 a.m.–6 p.m;
1 October–30 April, 11 a.m.–6 p.m.

ADMISSION: 1250 Iskr (about £6). Children under 13 in
company of adults free.

ITALY

BORA MUSEUM, TRIESTE

If you thought only the British were obsessed with the weather, there is an entire museum in Italy that is devoted to one particular wind. The bora is a cold, dry and often blustery north-easterly wind that blows down the Adriatic coast particularly in winter. Bora gusts in Trieste can reach 90 mph or more, ripping off tiles from roofs, overturning cars and forcing pedestrians to cling to the ropes and railings that have been installed in the more exposed areas to prevent people being blown under vehicles or into the sea. The wind has been known to last for an entire month in Trieste without a significant lull. Given its powers of destruction, you might expect the Italians to curse the bora, but instead they have chosen to celebrate its very existence by creating a museum in its honour, the *Museo della Bora*.

Located in the Wind House or *Magazzino dei Venti*, the Bora Museum of Trieste contains a wealth of historical books, archives and audiovisual material relating to the bora, which has been described as the most famous citizen of Trieste. A series of photographs illustrates what it can do to an unwary umbrella, while a selection of songs and poems pays tribute to the ill wind. In the Hall of Wind, visitors can experience first-hand what it is like to be on the receiving end of a blast from the bora. You can even pose in front of pictures of choppy seas as you watch your hat disappear in the general direction of Rome. Elsewhere, the archives of the Polli family present the work of Professor Silvio Polli, regarded by many as the world's leading expert on the bora. So that other winds do not feel left out, a separate section focuses on winds of the world, with demonstrations of wind-testing instruments and promises of 'an amusing collection of winds of different geographical areas in personalised containers.' These are cans of wind; in other words, they are empty cans. The curator also vows that nobody leaves the museum without having learned to build a simple windmill.

Combining fun and education, the museum may be small, but it is expanding all the time to cater for the locals' love/hate relationship with the howling gusts that sweep down from Slovenia. So the next time you hear a native of Trieste complaining about the wind, it might not be the spaghetti carbonara – it might be the bora.

ADDRESS: Via Belpoggio 9, 34124 Trieste, Italy

TEL: +39 040 307478

EMAIL: museobora@iol.it

WEBSITE: www.museobora.org

OPEN: By appointment.

ADMISSION: Free

LITTLE MUSEUM OF THE HOLY SOULS IN PURGATORY, ROME

The Catholic Church teaches that after death, souls go to purgatory to be purified of any remaining sins before eventually advancing to heaven. Depending on how sinful they have been, their stay in this 'halfway house' may be lengthy, but can be speeded up by the prayers of the loved ones they have left behind on Earth. By all accounts, purgatory isn't a particularly nice place, but it's not quite as bad as hell. So a bit like Luton.

Victor Jouet, a French missionary priest, decided to build a small purgatory museum after a fire in 1897 destroyed a section of the original *Chiesa del Sacro Cuore del Suffragio* (Church of the Sacred Heart of the Suffrage) on the banks of the Tiber in Rome, leaving behind in the burning walls of the altar the scorched image of a face that Father Jouet believed to be a soul trapped in purgatory. Thereafter he seemed to equate most fire damage with purgatory, and soon built up quite a collection of charred relics.

Located in a hallway towards the back of the rebuilt church, the *Piccolo Museo del Purgatorio* (Little Museum of the Holy Souls in Purgatory) amounts to a single wall-mounted glass case displaying a collection of around twenty Bibles, prayer books and articles of clothing said to have been singed by the hands of souls in purgatory. The scorched handprints and other burn marks are claimed to be the result of souls begging their living loved ones to pray for them just a little bit harder. Or they could just be stuff that has caught fire for no other reason than that fires happen, especially when there are lots of candles around. Among the items on show is the nightcap of a man who discovered his deceased wife's handprints on it asking him to pray for her. You can also see a book belonging to a woman whose dead mother-in-law supposedly appeared before her thirty years later in a vision and asked for two masses in her honour. After her wish was granted, her handprint was found on the book as a gesture of thanks. Further along, a burn mark on the apron of a Sister Herendorps was apparently made in 1696 by the hand of a fellow nun who had died of the plague fifty-nine years earlier. It certainly makes you think . . . or not. In fact, you may not believe any of these stories, but when in Rome . . .

Father Jouet died in the museum's only room in 1912, surrounded by his treasures, but his collection lives on. The museum is open whenever the church is, but once inside you may need to ask for directions, because its presence is not widely advertised. Just don't strike a match to see where you are going.

ADDRESS: Lungotevere Prati 12, 00193 Rome, Italy

TEL: +39 066 880 6517

OPEN: Daily, 9 a.m.–12.30 p.m., 5–7 p.m.

ADMISSION: Free

LITHUANIA

DEVILS' MUSEUM, KAUNAS

Lithuanian art collector Antanas Žmuidzinavičius (1876–1966) had a thing about devils, and on his death a memorial museum was established in his former home so that his satanic artefacts could be shown to a wider audience. At the time his collection amounted to only 260 sculptures, but, boosted by donations of Satan-related items from visitors (many of whom were only too keen to get rid of them), the collection grew so large that in 1982 a separate three-storey extension was built. Today the Devils' Museum (or Žmuidzinavičius Museum) houses more than 3,000 exhibits, among them paintings, sculptures, carvings and carnival masks depicting Satan, and even twigs that are shaped like him. It claims to be the largest collection of devils in a single place in the whole world, comfortably eclipsing the 2016 National Bankers Association Convention.

Some of the representations of Old Nick are from ancient folk myths, while others express modern political ideas. One sculpture shows Hitler and Stalin as devils performing a dance of death over the playground of Lithuania littered with human bones. There are also references to the devilish influence of alcohol and music, which may strike a chord if your idea of hell is being forced to watch *The X Factor*.

The first floor of the museum is devoted to Lithuanian devils, some with traditional horns and tail, but others in more human form, because in Lithuanian folklore the Devil is often a positive character, described as a smart, wealthy, cheerful individual who simply wants to get married and make friends. On the second floor are some of the devils given to the museum by people convinced that the presence of such statues in their homes was bringing them bad luck. There are also pebbles and other random items that appear to bear an image of the Devil, in the same way that the face of Jesus supposedly pops up regularly in wall stains, on toast, or in the residue of frying pans. A selection of novelty devils features plates, nutcrackers, pipes and ashtrays, because with all those heating bills, even Satan needs some income. The third floor is reserved for foreign devils and the superstitions attached to them. Russian peasants used to be terrified of using public bathhouses, as it was the only occasion when they removed their prayer belts, thereby leaving them vulnerable to the Devil. Before taking off their clothes, it was always a good idea to check that he wasn't hiding behind the towel rack.

The museum is decorated in devilish black and red, and the admission fee is modest, so you don't have to sell your soul to get in.

ADDRESS: V. Putvinskio g. 64, Kaunas 44211, Lithuania

TEL: +370 37 221587

EMAIL: mkc.velniai@takas.lt

WEBSITE: www.muziejai.lt

OPEN: Tuesday–Sunday, 11 a.m.–5 p.m., except Thursday, 11 a.m.–7 p.m. Closed national holidays.

ADMISSION: 1.74 euros

NETHERLANDS

RED LIGHT SECRETS, MUSEUM OF PROSTITUTION, AMSTERDAM

On a romantic trip to Amsterdam, you might struggle to persuade your partner that a visit to the Museum of Prostitution is an essential item on the itinerary. Yet in its own way this small educational museum offers an intriguing snapshot of the world's oldest profession, and one which has been an integral part of Amsterdam's history for hundreds of years. With prostitution tolerated in the Netherlands during the second half of the twentieth century (it was finally legalised in 2000), the city became an unlikely Mecca for curious tourists.

Located just a five-minute walk from the Central Station, in a former brothel in the heart of the infamous red light district, Red Light Secrets, which opened in 2014, allows visitors the opportunity to take a peek inside the hidden, shadowy world of prostitution. On any given evening, thousands stroll down the narrow canalside streets gazing at the lingerie-clad women posing in the front windows, but few have any idea about how the district operates on a business level. A short film shows the work of the various people who assist the prostitutes, cleaning their rooms, doing their laundry or supplying them with food and drink, while the women sit in the window waiting for the next customer.

The tour takes in a typical sex worker's room with all the expected accessories – strong, low bed, lubricants, sex toys and condoms – but no perfume because, as one guide explains, 'the smell rubs off on a man's clothes and he has problems with his wife when he gets home.' A wall of quotations from sex workers gives an idea of their true feelings about their job. 'It's not for the faint-hearted,' writes one, while another laments, 'It makes me feel lonely – my mother doesn't know what I do.' Another exhibit lists items that customers have apparently left behind when visiting a prostitute. Watches, wallets and phones will come as no surprise, but one poor man forgot to pick up his dentures. He might have had some explaining to do when he got home. Before venturing back out on to the street, visitors can write down their own sexual secrets in a mock-up confessional booth.

Allow around forty minutes for the tour, the highlight of which is to have your photograph taken sitting in the window just like a real sex worker. It may be best, however, not to use it as your profile picture on LinkedIn.

ADDRESS: Oudezijds Achterburgwal 60, 1012 DP
Amsterdam, Netherlands

TEL: +31 20 662 5300

WEBSITE: www.redlightsecrets.com

OPEN: Daily, 11 a.m.–midnight.

ADMISSION: 10 euros at the door. If you book online, you receive a twenty per cent discount.

EUROPE

TORTURE MUSEUM, AMSTERDAM

In the heart of vibrant Amsterdam near the flower market stands an altogether more sinister attraction: a dark, dungeon-like museum that is home to an extensive range of more than forty European torture devices, including horrific thumbscrews, skull crushers, the chair of the Spanish Inquisition and, of course, that old staple of French public entertainment, the guillotine.

Those with a fascination for medieval history, or who think the days of public executions and trial by ordeal were 'the good old days', will find plenty of interest here. The iron maiden, from which the rock band took their name, was an iron cabinet (built to house a human prisoner) that had sharp spikes on its interior, so that in whichever direction the occupant leaned, his or her flesh would be pierced. Even more gruesome was the Judas chair. The victim was placed in a harness above a pyramid-shaped seat, the point of which was inserted into the anus or vagina. As the person was lowered slowly by ropes, the pain from the intense stretching of the orifice usually produced the desired confession. The alternative was an agonising death from either infection or impalement. The scold's bridle was often used to punish and humiliate women suspected of being witches or gossips. First recorded in Scotland in 1567, it took the form of an iron muzzle fitted over the head, studded with sharp spikes so as to inflict pain whenever the offender moved her tongue, making speaking impossible. Another favourite was the Catherine wheel or breaking wheel, a large wooden wagon wheel to which the condemned man was tied in order to be bludgeoned with an iron cudgel until his limbs broke. Death invariably followed within a couple of days. The wheel was still being used as a means of execution in parts of Germany in the early nineteenth century. Various racks and stocks are also on display, but while many of the items are genuine antiques, others are modern reconstructions of medieval devices.

A series of illustrations cranks up the fear factor, notably one of a naked man hanging from his ankles like a wishbone and being sawn in half lengthwise. It makes you grateful that the worst torture you can encounter in modern-day Europe is a stale baguette or the Eurovision Song Contest. On that note, one of the museum's most ingenious devices is the flute of shame, which was designed to punish bad musicians. The flute-like instrument was hung around the neck of the offender, whose fingers were then clamped tightly to it for several days, rendering him unable to use his hands and, more to the point, unable to play. The museum offers guided tours for schools, not to give kids ideas for exacting revenge on their maths teacher but to educate them on the cruelty of the past and the pitfalls of capital punishment.

ADDRESS: Singel 449, 1012 WP Amsterdam, Netherlands

TEL: +31 20 320 6642

EMAIL: info@torturemuseum.com

WEBSITE: www.torturemuseum.nl

OPEN: Daily, 10 a.m.–11 p.m.

ADMISSION: 7 euros adults; 2.50 euros children.

NORWAY

MINI BOTTLE GALLERY, OSLO

Whereas Denmark is happy to show off miniature ships squeezed into full-sized bottles, its Scandinavian neighbour prefers everyday objects stuffed into miniature bottles. Oslo's Mini Bottle Gallery – the only one of its kind in the world – boasts a collection of 55,000 miniature bottles exhibited in fifty different installations in a three-storey building. Their contents range from fruit and berries to worms and dead mice.

The museum was opened in 2003 by Christian Ringnes Jr, a member of a long-established Norwegian brewing family, who had started collecting miniature bottles at the age of seven after receiving one from his father as a present. With his father bringing back more bottles from business trips abroad, Christian's enthusiasm continued unabated, even into marriage. His wife Denise was none too pleased to find that vast areas of their first apartment were given over to miniature bottles, and it is said that she wore an especially broad grin on the day when some of the shelving collapsed and left part of the collection in pieces. He packed the surviving bottles away for safekeeping until, in 1996, he purchased a building in the heart of Oslo's museum district and hit upon the idea of using it to showcase them.

The eccentric owner, who has been known to wear a crown of miniature bottles, has created a decidedly quirky museum. As you would expect, miniature bottles are everywhere – even in light fittings, beneath a Scotsman's kilt and in a mock-up of a brothel. There are small bottles in the shape of mermaids, ballroom dancers, a flamingo, Charlie Chaplin and Sylvester the cat. Many of the bottles contain beers and spirits from various parts of the world, and there is a 'Wall of Fragrance' where visitors can attempt to identify different drinks by their smells. They then descend a slide to the 'Room of Horror', home to plastic skeletons and liquor bottles containing an assortment of dead wildlife. The horror theme extends to the men's toilets, where only the brave will dare to use the urinal with its gothic bowl in the guise of a devilish mouth with razor-sharp teeth. By contrast, the ladies' bathroom is so pink even Barbara Cartland might have shied away from it. To round off your visit, you can have your picture taken standing in a large bottle of Absolut vodka, although sadly the bottle is empty.

ADDRESS: Kirkegata 10, 0153 Oslo, Norway

TEL: +47 2335 7960

EMAIL: post@minibottlegallery.com

WEBSITE: www.minibottlegallery.com

OPEN: Saturday, Sunday, noon–4 p.m.

ADMISSION: 85 NOK (about £6.50, adults; 35 NOK (about £2.70) children.

POLAND

NEON MUSEUM, WARSAW

During the 1960s and 1970s, the largely drab buildings that predominated in many Polish cities were lit up with banks of neon signs promoting products, dancehalls, cinemas, hotels, restaurants, cocktail bars and railway stations. These signs, designed by some of Poland's leading architects, were seen as a symbol of economic success and as part of the country's cultural fabric. The communist government of the time even embarked on a planned programme of 'neonisation', whereby neon signs were installed along the entire length of urban streets, carefully co-ordinated in size and colour and placed in such a manner that they did not obscure one another. However, in the post-communist era many of the objects associated with that period were destroyed. Buildings were demolished, and the neon signs were either tossed into skips or left to rust. Happily, photographer Ilona Karwiska and graphic designer David Hill realised the social significance of these illuminated artworks, and in 2012 they managed to rescue a sizeable number for display in a museum celebrating the glorious history of Polish Cold War neon.

With over 100 neon signs and 1,000 neon letters, the *Neon Muzeum* has the largest collection of neon signs anywhere in Europe, and during the European Museum Nights event of 2014 no fewer than 16,000 visitors passed through its doors in a single night. Some of the signs display a jollity not readily associated with communism – a neon mermaid announcing the location of a public library, and a cat in boots advertising shoes. You half expect to see a neon sign depicting Leonid Brezhnev's dancing eyebrows.

Situated in a renovated factory, the museum is also home to a vast archive of documents, blueprints, plans and photographs relating to the history and manufacture of the signs. If you have ever wondered why neon signs come in so many different colours, it is down to the shade of the tube or the mix of the gases inside. You see, there is a lot to be learned from this peek behind the Iron Curtain.

ADDRESS:	Budynek 55, Soho Factory, Mińska 25, 03-808 Warsaw, Poland
TEL:	+48 665 71 16 35
EMAIL:	info@neonmuzeum.org
WEBSITE:	www.neonmuzeum.org
OPEN:	Wednesday–Sunday, noon–5 p.m.
ADMISSION:	10 zloty (£1.70) adults; 8 zloty (£1.30) children.

RUSSIA

KUNSTKAMERA, ST PETERSBURG

The oldest of all Russian museums, the vast *Kunstkamera* (also known as the Museum of Anthropology and Ethnography) is home to some two million items, many collected by that connoisseur of the obscure, Tsar Peter the Great. When Peter decided to move the country's capital from Moscow to the emerging city of St Petersburg (which he modestly named after himself), he arranged for his private collection of oddities to go with him. In 1714, these collections were displayed in rooms in the Summer Palace under the name of the *Kunstkamera*, which translates as 'cabinet of art'. There, Peter assembled anything and anyone that he considered to be a freak of nature. Exhibits included a man without genital organs, a child with two heads, a lamb with eight legs, another with three eyes, a sheep with two tongues, a calf with two heads, a deformed human foetus, and a pickled phallus, the last generously donated by the King of Prussia. Peter enjoyed nothing more than wandering among the jars of abnormal specimens, all of which were pickled in alcohol, and his provincial governors were offered handsome rewards for sending in suitable curiosities. He went so far as to issue an edict that all malformed, stillborn infants in Russia should be sent to him for possible inclusion in his collection. As caretaker of the museum he appointed a dwarf who had only two fingers on each hand and two toes on each foot, and who was well aware that when he eventually died, he too would be stuffed and pickled and put on display.

Peter's goal was not just to provide an entertaining freak show: he wanted to educate, by reducing the climate of superstition that prevailed among the Russian people. By cataloguing malformed infants and medical abnormalities as quirks of nature, he reasoned, he would be able to quell the widely held belief that they were caused by demons and monsters. Some of his subjects would have taken a lot of convincing.

As the collection expanded, it was forced to move to larger premises, and thankfully many of Peter's curiosities are still on display, including the giant skeleton and outsized heart of a 7-foot-2-inch Frenchman named Nicholas Bourgeois. In those days, collecting dwarfs and giants was fashionable in Europe, and after spotting Bourgeois at a fair in Calais, Peter appointed him as his bodyguard. When Bourgeois died at the age of forty-two, Peter kept his skeleton at the *Kunstkamera*, but the skull was lost in a fire in 1747 and later replaced by another skull. According to legend, the skeleton still roams the halls of the museum every night in search of his real head.

However, the prize specimen at the *Kunstkamera* is the decapitated head of Willem Mons, the ill-fated lover of Peter's wife. Although Peter himself enjoyed the luxury of countless mistresses, he did not take kindly to his wife Catherine being unfaithful in return, so when he discovered that she had been having a romantic liaison with the imperial chamberlain, he had Mons publicly drawn and quartered, and his head chopped off and inserted in a large jar of alcohol. Ironically, Mons was the brother of Peter's long-time mistress, Anna. It is said that before being transferred to the *Kunstkamera*, the jar and its gruesome contents were kept at Catherine's bedside table to remind her of her folly. The pickled preserves shock today's visitors just as much as they did in the eighteenth century, so pregnant women might be advised to give a wide berth to the babies in jars.

ADDRESS:	University Embankment 3, 199034 St Petersburg, Russia
TEL:	+7 812 328 1412
EMAIL:	info@kunstkamera.ru
WEBSITE:	www.kunstkamera.ru
OPEN:	Daily except Monday, 11 a.m.–7 p.m. Also closed on the last Tuesday of each month.
ADMISSION:	250 rubles (£2.50) adults; 50 rubles (50p) children, students and seniors.

SPAIN

MUSEUM OF FUNERAL CARRIAGES, BARCELONA

Barcelona is widely regarded as one of Europe's most vibrant cities, but there is one spot that is deathly quiet: the *Museu de Carrosses Fúnebres*, Europe's first and only public display of funeral carriages. The museum was created in 1970 and until 2013 was housed in the basement of a local funeral home, before moving to the Montjuic Cemetery high on the hill above the city.

The collection comprises thirteen funeral carriages – some dating back to the eighteenth century – plus three more modern motor hearses (among them a splendid silver Buick) and six horse-drawn coaches designed to carry relatives of the deceased to the church and cemetery. One such coach, windowless and lined entirely in black fabric, was used to transport the widow. Its gloomy air was calculated to induce a state of mourning, although as the widow she really should not have needed much encouragement to look sad – at least not in public. Privately she might have been doing cartwheels.

The carriages vary in grandeur according to the status of the deceased. The basic carriage, known as the 'spider', was the most commonly used, while the ornate Imperial Carriage was reserved for the burials of emperors and public figures. The white carriages were used for the funerals of children, virgins and religious figures. Many of the vehicles in the museum are manned by ghoulish dummies dressed in period costume, presumably for the benefit of visitors who want to believe they are at a real funeral. For light relief, there is a photo gallery showing some of the major funerals to have been held in Barcelona.

Next to the museum is Spain's foremost funeral library, which contains nearly 4,000 publications devoted to the funeral customs of various civilisations from prehistoric times up to the present day. Fascinating it may be, but for reading on the beach Volume One of *The History of Catalan Funerals* is no substitute for a Jackie Collins paperback.

ADDRESS:	Cementerio de Montjuic, Carrer de la Mare de Déu de Port 56–58, 08038 Barcelona, Spain
TEL:	+34 93 484 1999
OPEN:	Wednesday–Sunday, 10 a.m.–2 p.m.
ADMISSION:	Free

REZOLA CEMENT MUSEUM, SAN SEBASTIAN

Of all the attractions in Spain – golden beaches, Michelin-starred restaurants, spectacular festivals – a visit to a cement museum would be fairly low down on most people's list. In terms of appeal it ranks on a par with watching paint – or indeed cement – dry. Nor does this establishment make any attempt to dress up such an unpromising concept with an enticing exterior. Instead, its solid grey concrete blocks look like the entrance to a 1960s-built city centre underground car park. The architecture could never be mistaken for Gaudi.

Located in the suburbs of San Sebastian, the *Museum Cemento Rezola* gamely celebrates the heritage of José Maria Rezola Gaztañaga who, taking advantage of the copious limestone deposits in the region, opened his first cement factory in 1850 in a converted flour mill. Cementos Rezola went on to become one of the major players in the Basque industrial sector and the museum, opened in 2000 to mark the company's 150th anniversary, explains in precise detail the process of making cement. As mere words cannot do it justice, audio-visuals, simulations and interactive modules are utilised to enhance the visitor's understanding of cement and its role in modern civilisation. No block is left unturned. If you ever thought cement manufacture was dull and boring, you were probably right.

ADDRESS: Avenida Añorga 36, Donostia-San Sebastian
20018, Spain

TEL: +34 943 364192

EMAIL: info@museumcementorezola.org

WEBSITE: museumcementorezola.org

OPEN: Tuesday–Sunday, 10.30 a.m.–2 p.m.; Saturday, 10 a.m.–2 p.m., 5 p.m.–8 p.m. Closed Monday.

ADMISSION: Free

SWEDEN

SURSTRÖMMING MUSEUM, SKEPPSMALEN

One might wonder why anyone of sound mind would wish to open a museum dedicated solely to one of the world's foulest-smelling foods, but that is exactly what the Swedes have done with the *Fiskevistet Surströmmingmuseet*, their shrine to *surström-ming*. Swedish for 'soured herring', *surströmming* is a fermented Baltic Sea herring so pungent that when a can of it smashes to the floor in a supermarket, they generally evacuate the store. Its odour has been likened to that of eggs rotting in open sewage drains. It is almost always eaten outside – in fact, it is illegal to take *surströmming* into apartment buildings in Stockholm – because its stench will linger for days, like skunk spray. In 1981, a German landlord evicted a tenant without notice for spreading *surströmming* brine in the staircase of the apartment building. The landlord was taken to court, where he successfully proved his case by opening a can of *surströmming* in the courtroom. The court concluded that it 'had convinced itself that the disgusting smell of the fish brine far exceeded the degree that fellow tenants in the building could be expected to tolerate.' In 2014, a Japanese study declared a newly opened can of *surströmming* to be the worst-smelling food on the planet. The Swedes considered it an accolade.

Cans of *surströmming* have also been known to explode, prompting British Airways and Air France to ban it from flights. Acting in sympathy, Stockholm's international airport withdrew it from sale. In 2014, a fire at a Swedish warehouse containing 1,000 cans of *surströmming* caused explosions that lasted for six hours, launching cans to all points of the surrounding area.

It has been a staple of northern Swedish cuisine for over 500 years. Back in the sixteenth century, it was supplied as army rations to Swedish troops fighting the Thirty Years War. Foreign conscripts and those Swedish soldiers unfamiliar with *surströmming* flatly refused to eat it, but at least its very presence probably helped keep the enemy at bay.

When selecting a location for the world's first fermented herring museum, the Swedes at least put it way up in the north of the country in about as isolated a spot as could be found. It opened its doors (but only slightly) in 2005.

The exhibition is housed in two locations, where you can discover more than you ever wanted to know about herring. In the boathouse, you can learn about the life of a herring fisherman, fermented herring traditions, how herring communicate with each other (they fart, which probably explains a lot), and some hearty drinking songs. There is also a sniffing box where you can familiarise yourself with the aroma. Once your stomach has stopped turning, over in the *Fiskevistet* restaurant a video gives advice on how to prepare and eat *surströmming* without throwing up, while articles on the walls chronicle the chequered history of fermented herring. If you're curious about actually trying *surströmming*, the bad news is that it's on the menu.

ADDRESS: Fiskevistet Surströmmingmuseet, Skagsudde,
Skeppsmalen 891 96, Arnäsvall, Sweden

TEL: + 46 0660 256019

WEBSITE: fiskevistet.se

OPEN: Daily, mid-June to mid-August, 11 a.m.–6 p.m.
Other times by appointment.

ADMISSION: 30 SEK (about £2.25)

TURKEY

CHEZ GALIP HAIR MUSEUM, AVANOS

Since 3000 BC the town of Avanos in the Cappadocia region of Turkey has been renowned for its high-quality earthenware, but for the last thirty-five years it has also become famous for an attraction of a different kind: a hair museum filled with locks from more than 16,000 women.

The museum was created by local potter Galip Korukçu in 1979, and is located in a cave beneath his pottery shop. The story goes that when one of his female friends had to leave Avanos, she left him a piece of her hair as a memento. For some strange reason, this inspired other lady customers in his shop to chop off a lock of their own hair and present it to him, along with their names and addresses. Before long, the assorted clippings – blonde, redhead, brunette, black, and even green – were lining the walls and ceiling of the basement to create a fully-fledged museum. The addresses enable Galip to contact his old customers: twice a year, ten of the hair samples are chosen at random, and the women to whom they once belonged are invited back to his studio for a pottery workshop and to stay in his guest house for a week – all free of charge. The really keen donors also attach a passport photo to their lock of hair.

Even though the samples were given willingly, it has to be said that the overall effect of the hair cave is decidedly creepy, like the

125

sort of serial killer's trophy room you would see in an episode of *CSI*. Women visiting the shop are not obliged to donate a piece of their hair for display in the museum, but if they wish to, scissors, Sellotape, pens, paper and drawing pins are provided. No matter how luxuriant their mane, men will not be considered. Ironically, the website's photographs of Galip at work suggest the one thing he really needs is a haircut.

ADDRESS: 24 Avanos Nevşehir, Yukan, 110 Sk., 50500 Avanos/Nevşehir, Turkey

TEL: +90 384 511 4240 or +90 384 511 5758

WEBSITE: www.chezgalip.com

OPEN: Daily, 10 a.m.–8 p.m.

ADMISSION: Free

AFRICA

SOUTH AFRICA

KWAZULU MUTI MUSEUM OF MAN AND SCIENCE, JOHANNESBURG

This medicinal museum/shop in downtown Johannesburg has been around for over half a century, and stocks nearly 2,000 dried herbs prescribed by traditional healers, as well as witch doctors' favourite animal part remedies like monkey skulls and dried crocodile feet.

You can also buy tyre sandals, walking sticks, knobkerries (wooden clubs), beads, Zulu pots and drums, and make an appointment with the resident *sangoma* (a spiritual healer) who, for a small fee, will throw the bones for you –a technique used to seek the opinion of the ancestors, rather like a doctor asking for a second opinion from an eminent, but unfortunately dead, surgeon. According to the position in which the animal bones land, the *sangoma* will be able to suggest an appropriate cure for your condition in the store. You don't get that in Boots.

Even if you don't buy anything, the weird sights (including ostrich feet dangling from the ceiling) and smells are something to behold.

So if, while on holiday in South Africa, you do happen to go down with an ailment or curse for which the only known cure is a dose of powdered dried crocodile feet, it is comforting to know that someone else has already done the groundwork, and that it won't be you who has to go to the trouble of relieving an understandably peeved crocodile of its limbs.

ADDRESS: 14 Diagonal St., Johannesburg CBD, South Africa

TEL: +27 11 836 4470

OPEN: Monday–Friday, 7.30 a.m.–5 p.m.; Saturday, 7.30 a.m.–1.30 p.m.

ADMISSION: Free

SHOE HOUSE MUSEUM, MPUMALANGA

Although it is located far out in the magnificent countryside of Mpumalanga Province, over twelve miles north of the town of Ohrigstad, you are unlikely to miss the Shoe House Museum – because the building itself is constructed in the shape of a giant lace-up shoe.

The two-storey Shoe House was built in 1990 by artist and hotel-ier Ron Van Zyl as a quirky home for his wife Yvonne, and houses a small museum showcasing Van Zyl's rock and wood carvings and featuring a history of the Ohrigstad Valley, an area once ravaged by malaria. Exhibits include a human skull, and a clay pot believed to have been used by a local witch doctor during the Iron Age.

As well as the museum, the shoe contains an art gallery, curio shop and tea garden, plus the curious Alpha Omega Caves, which, for an additional admission fee, are entered via a door near the heel. Apparently the caves were built to specifications that came to Van Zyl in a vision. The seven man-made underground rooms take the visitor on a mysterious journey through the spiritual world, which will either be creepy or uplifting depending on your point of view. The final room is a small chapel where weddings can be held. Getting married beneath the sole of a shoe would seem to be a sure-fire recipe for a life as a downtrodden spouse. The shoe also operates as a guest house, with a number of chalets located at the rear. The contents of the Shoe House Museum may not be particularly remarkable, but the building in which they are housed definitely is.

ADDRESS: R36 Panorama Route, near Ohrigstad,
Mpumalanga, 1122 South Africa

TEL: +27 13 238 0304

WEBSITE: theshoe.org

OPEN: Daily, 9 a.m.–4 p.m.

ADMISSION: (for museum) R3 (about 12p); (for caves) R50 (about £2).

ASIA

CHINA

BEIJING MUSEUM OF TAP WATER, BEIJING

There are few more compelling topics of conversation than water pipes through the ages . . . if you happen to be at a convention of civil engineers. The rest of us tend only to think about water pipes when they burst and land us with a hefty call-out fee from a plumber. You know it's going to cost you more at the weekend when he turns up in his Bentley instead of his van. Supplying clean, running water to major cities has long been a major challenge, nowhere more so than in Beijing, where they are so proud of their achievements that they have established a museum to celebrate the history of the city's tap water.

The Jingshi Tap Water Company Ltd was founded in 1908 on the orders of Empress Cixi, who wanted an efficient system of pipelines to tackle the fires that regularly blighted the city, including one that had damaged her palace the previous year. Built in 2000 on the site of the original water plant at Dongzhimen, just outside the city gates, the museum traces the evolution of Beijing's underground water pipe network with the aid of maps, documents and designs, a display of old water meters, exhibits explaining the complexities of water purification, a miniature working model of a tap water filtration system, the correct procedure for water quality monitoring, and, for those who don't know what a man inspecting a pipe looks like, some photos of a man inspecting a pipe. Initially the city's residents were highly suspicious of water that travelled underground and preferred to use wells, so to win them round, the water plant embarked on a vast advertising campaign, which involved putting up posters across the city explaining how safe tap water was. They also offered incentives such as free tastings and discounts for the elderly. At first, the new chlorinated water was not supplied directly into people's homes. Instead, citizens could either buy tickets and draw water from the new outdoor public taps that had been installed across Beijing, or arrange for it to be delivered to their homes in wooden buckets from water carts. Water rationing was still commonplace after the Second World War, and photographs of the public water station show 'tap keepers' collecting coupons in exchange for rationed portions of water.

The excitement derived from a visit to the museum may be tempered by the fact that most of the indoor captions are in Chinese only. However, an English translation does appear on signs labelling some of the outdoor exhibits, including those on vintage pumps, which warn visitors not to drink the water. For even after marvelling at how the twenty million people of Beijing receive their tap water, you will still need to seek out the nearest bottle of Buxton or Highland Spring (other bottled waters are available) because, ironically, the main lesson to be learned from the Beijing Museum of Tap Water is that the tap water in Beijing is not safe to drink.

ADDRESS: 6A Dongzhimenwai Beidajie, Dongcheng
District, Beijing, China

TEL: +86 10 6465 0787

OPEN: Wednesday–Sunday, 9 a.m.–4 p.m.

ADMISSION: 5 yuan (about 50p)

INDIA

SUDHA CARS MUSEUM, HYDERABAD

There are car museums all over the world, containing vehicles large and small, old and new, sporty and sedate – but none quite like this one. For these exhibits would be more at home in *Wacky Races*, as they include a dazzling array of crazy cars in the shape of everyday objects: a toilet, a high-heeled shoe, a cigarette, a hamburger, a dining table, and even a driveable condom, the ultimate safety car. There are more than 700 vehicles in total, all built by the intrepid Kanyaboyina Sudhakar. It is fair to say that when he drives along the streets of Hyderabad in his home-made contraptions, heads turn.

He has always been fascinated by vehicles of all shapes and sizes. 'When I was young, my friends used to go to the movies, but I used to skip them and go to the mechanic shop. I designed my first car when I was fourteen, using materials I collected from local junkyards. I was in high school, so I had little money. So I used to visit a couple of junkyards near my house and pick up random stuff from cars lying there.' Many of the parts used in his fanciful designs have been retrieved from scrapyards. He has a particular fondness for buses, which led to him building what he claims is the world's smallest working double-decker London bus.

As his collection grew, in 2010 Sudhakar decided to open it up as a museum, which now attracts thousands of auto enthusiasts every year to come and stare in wonder at cars in the guise of a camera, a book, a handbag, a cricket bat, a football, a sofa, a coffee mug, a suitcase and a computer. The last named is, as might be expected, a hard drive. Their top speed might be modest, but in Indian cities nothing on the road moves quickly. In 2015, he unveiled a stationary, two-storey, 26-foot-tall, 50-foot-long replica vintage cár, modelled on a 1922 Ford Tourer. The wheels are nine feet in diameter and there is a giant chess-board on the roof, which is reached via a staircase. It took him three years to build.

Sudhakar has also built a number of barmy bikes, ranging in size from the gigantic to the tiny, and in 2005 earned a Guinness World Record for creating the world's largest tricycle, a 41-foot-high monstrosity that he gallantly rode himself. One of his most imaginative designs is his fountain pen motorbike, a slim green machine fitted with a 60 cc engine and with a top speed of 37 mph. You could just picture Dick Dastardly perched on top, riding for dear life, nose pressed against the nib.

Sudhakar will put a set of wheels on just about anything (which must be a concern to the animals in the nearby city zoo), whether it be a Christmas tree or a full-sized snooker table. Each vehicle costs less than £2,000 to manufacture. The bad news is that none are for sale.

ADDRESS: 19–5-15/1/D, Bahadurpura, Hyderabad, Telangana
500264, India

TEL: +91 40 2446 3376

EMAIL: sudhacarsmuseum@rediffmail.com

WEBSITE: sudhacars.com

OPEN: Daily, 9.30 a.m.–6.30 p.m.

ADMISSION: 200 rupees (about £2)

SULABH INTERNATIONAL MUSEUM OF TOILETS, NEW DELHI

Just as Japan would be the natural place for a photography museum, and Spain the obvious choice for a bullfighting museum, there is a certain logic in the International Museum of Toilets being located in the city that brought the world 'Delhi belly'.

The museum was established in 1992 by Dr Bindeshwar Pathak, who twenty-two years earlier had founded Sulabh Sanitation to address the alarming state of sanitation in India, where the practice of open defecation and use of bucket toilets was all too common. It has exhibits from fifty countries, arranged in sections for Ancient, Medieval and Modern, covering the history of toilet devices from 2500 BC to the present day. Looking at some primitive latrines – nothing more than communal holes in the ground – gives new meaning to the term 'trench warfare'.

There are elegant gold and silver toilets used by Roman emperors, a reproduction of the toilet that Louis XIV of France had built into his throne, into which to save time he would defecate while holding court, a reproduction English medieval commode in the form of a treasure chest, a Las Vegas loo with advertising for a bakery on the lid, a toilet that doubles up as a table, a modern electric toilet that burns human waste into ash, and an eighteenth-century French toilet cunningly camouflaged as a small bookcase. This disguise may have been useful for concealing embarrassing functions, but would have been a nightmare for any visitor suddenly caught short in the chateau library.

Look out, too, for an American two-storey toilet from the 1920s. The top storey was reserved for management, the lower for employees. This was, of course, by no means the last time that workers were dumped on by management. There is also information on a toilet developed in Chicago that had a buttock-stimulating mechanism to overcome cases of constipation.

In addition to the chamber pots, decorated Victorian toilet seats, bidets and water closets you would expect to find, the museum risks causing a stink with toilet humour, by featuring a selection of potty-based poetry, jokes and cartoons.

ADDRESS:	Sulabh Bhawan, Palam Dabri Marg, Mahavir Enclave, Palam, New Delhi, DL 110045, India
TEL:	+91 11 2503 1518
WEBSITE:	www.sulabhtoiletmuseum.org
OPEN:	Daily (except national holidays), 1 November–31 March, 10.30 a.m.–5 p.m.; 1 April–31 October, 10 a.m.–5 p.m.
ADMISSION:	Free

JAPAN

MEGURO PARASITOLOGICAL MUSEUM, TOKYO

If your idea of a fun day out is to see the world's longest tapeworm and lots of other parasitic worms, crabs and bugs that are trying to burrow into your body and feed off your innards, then this is the place for you. It proudly claims to be the only museum in the world dedicated to parasitic disease, although, to put it into context, it is rather like opening the world's only Bubonic Plague theme park.

The record-busting 29-foot-long tapeworm was taken from the body of a forty-year-old Yokohama man, and was apparently caused by the patient eating too much sushi. It lived inside him for three months until he finally pooped it out. And he never felt a thing! Although the dead worm is coiled up in its display case (the room would struggle to accommodate it if stretched out), it is helpfully accompanied by a piece of ribbon of the same dimensions, which you can play with to get a feel of the tapeworm's alarming size. It may put you off sushi – or indeed any food – for some time.

It is one of around 300 parasites on display at the museum, which was established in 1953 with the private funds of a local doctor, Satoru Kamegai, who had become concerned about the growing number of parasites he was encountering as a result of the poor sanitation in post-war Japan. The second-floor displays are particularly cheery, depicting parasite life cycles and the symptoms they cause during human infection. This includes graphic photographs showing the severely distended testicles of the hapless human host of a tropical bug. A nearby jar contains the head of an unfortunate turtle whose tongue has been replaced by a parasite. On the same floor is the museum shop, which sells parasite-related T-shirts, key rings and greetings cards. That's one card you won't find in Clinton Cards: 'Hope your intestinal hookworm infestation is better.'

In the name of research, the museum actually collects and preserves 60,000 parasite specimens, and boasts 50,000 papers and 6,000 books on parasitic diseases. Luckily most of these are kept behind closed doors.

If you think there would be little interest in a parasite collection, you'd be wrong. For the museum is regularly packed, as dozens of Japanese people of all ages choose to spend their Saturday afternoons gawping at jars of formaldehyde and their gruesome contents. Incredibly, the museum is a popular venue for young dating couples, because what could be more romantic than holding hands and looking at a near thirty-foot tapeworm?

ADDRESS: 4-1-1 Shimomeguro, Meguro, Tokyo 153-0064, Japan

TEL: +81 3 3716 1264

WEBSITE: www.kiseichu.org

OPEN: Tuesday–Sunday, 10 a.m.–5 p.m.

ADMISSION: Free

MOMOFUKU ANDO INSTANT RAMEN MUSEUM, IKEDA

Without Momofuku Ando, the world would never have tasted Pot Noodle. Some might dispute whether this is necessarily a cause for celebration, but the Japanese clearly think so, and have honoured the inventor of Cup Noodles with his very own museum.

It was in 1958, after months of trial and error, that Ando marketed the first pack of instant noodles, Chicken Ramen, but it was another thirteen years before he came up with the idea of putting them in a waterproof polystyrene cup. Today around 100 billion cups and pots of instant noodles are sold annually worldwide.

The museum was established in 1999, and exhibits include a replica of the very shed behind his home in Ikeda where Ando, working alone for an entire year, during which he never took a day off and only ever slept four hours at night, finally perfected the manufacture of instant noodles by adding hot water. Visitors can sit in a theatre built in the shape of a giant noodle cup to watch videos of how he later had his brainwave about putting his noodles in Styrofoam. This came on a visit to the United States, where a prospective Chicken Ramen buyer, possessing neither noodle bowls nor chopsticks, tipped the noodles into a paper cup, added hot water and ate them with a fork. There is also a facility where, for 300 yen, you can create your own cup of noodles, designing the cup and selecting the ingredients from a list of pre-prepared flavours. For the more adventurous, there is even a kitchen area where you can make your own noodles, but this needs to be booked in advance.

A museum dedicated solely to instant noodles might be expected to have only limited appeal, but be warned: it can get very busy. Indeed, for students the world over, who have existed for four years eating little else, it is almost the equivalent of paradise.

ADDRESS: 8–25 Masumicho, Ikeda 563-0041, Osaka
Prefecture, Japan

TEL: +81 72 752 3484

OPEN: Daily except Tuesday, 9.30 a.m.–4 p.m.

ADMISSION: Free

MALAYSIA

MUSEUM OF ENDURING BEAUTY, MALACCA

Located on the third floor of the People's Museum, the Museum of Enduring Beauty chronicles some of the ways in which people from different cultures have over the centuries tried to make themselves look more attractive. If you are expecting just an exhibition of lipsticks, hair gels and nail polish, you'll be in for a nasty shock, because the emphasis here is on the more extreme measures people adopt in the name of beauty. Yes, we're talking neck stretching, lip stretching, tooth filing, foot binding and head moulding, all of which combine to give the impression that the 'enduring' in the title means 'suffering', as opposed to 'lasting'.

The museum opened in 1996, and every month attracts around 2,000 visitors who come to learn about scarification, tattooing and other body modification/mutilation practices, some of which date back thousands of years. Recoil in horror at the sight of the Padaung women of Thailand and Myanmar, who wear heavy brass rings around their necks from the age of five because elongated necks are supposed to be a sign of beauty. The weight of the rings pushes down the collarbone so that the neck appears to be up to 15 inches long – five times the length of the average woman's neck. No wonder they call them 'Giraffe Women'.

A clay sculpture depicts an African woman with a huge lip plate and stretched earlobes, while another display tells the story of Ethel Granger, an Englishwoman who, at one point in her life, had a waist measuring a mere 13 inches – barely enough room for her spine – but lived to the age of 77. As for tooth filing, anyone who is not actively campaigning to be the villain in the next James Bond movie should seriously think twice before subjecting themselves to it. The dangerous practice of foot binding to restrict the growth of children's feet was carried out in China for 1,000 years, continuing right up until the twentieth century. Western women may scoff at the folly of it all . . . but then go out on a Saturday night wearing painfully tight stilettos in which they can barely walk.

What with vajazzling, flesh hooks, breast implants, horn implants, forked tongues, cheek holes, and when even your granny splashes her pension money on a new tattoo, it seems that today we are going to yet more alarming lengths in our attempts to appear attractive. Whatever happened to just wearing a nice tie?

ADDRESS: Kota Road, Malacca 75000, Malaysia

TEL: +60 6282 6526

OPEN: Tuesday–Sunday, 9.30 a.m.–5 p.m.

ADMISSION: MYR 2 (30p) adults; MYR 0.50 (8p) children.

SOUTH KOREA

MANIKER MUSEUM OF CHICKEN ART, DONGDUCHEON

Have you ever been to an art gallery and thought, 'These paintings of water lilies, starry nights and enigmatic women are all very well, but all I really want to look at are works of art featuring chickens'? If so, then the Korean city of Dongducheon has the answer to your prayers: a museum in which every painting and sculpture features a chicken, thus making it one of the world's most exclusive art galleries.

Inside you will find more than 2,000 chicken art exhibits from all over the world – China, Japan, New Zealand, Germany, USA, Russia and Spain – in no particular pecking order. Paintings of roosters in their finest plumage adorn the walls, while display tables are full of chicken sculptures, chiefly in ceramic, metal, glass or wood, although there is also an Indian chicken carved from a coconut. The chickens here come in many guises: puppets, clocks, pieces of furniture, embroidery, tiles, jewellery, stamps, wine bottles, coins, lamps and rubbish bins. They have been collected over the years by Kim Cho Gang, a retired public health professor who, as you might suspect, is decidedly fowl-friendly.

So why the chicken? Well, Koreans traditionally have a very close relationship with the chicken, and not just in the kitchen. To ancient Koreans, the bird was a symbol of wealth and fertility, and when someone died, a *kkokdu*, a brightly painted wooden sculpture of a chicken, would decorate the coffin, because of the twelve animals in the Chinese zodiac, only the chicken possesses the wings necessary to accompany the dead between this world and the afterlife. One of the nuggets of chicken trivia you will pick up from your tour is that, because it rises early, the chicken is still seen by Koreans as a symbol of success. However, Kim felt that, despite its status in Korean culture, the chicken was no longer being fully appreciated. Someone needed to crow about it. 'I do not buy luxuries,' she has said. 'I don't buy cosmetics. I am only indulged in chickens.'

She opened her chicken art museum in Seoul in 2006, but at the start of 2012 it moved to the city of Dongducheon in the grounds of a chicken factory, thereby enabling visitors to enjoy the ultimate chicken experience: admire it, pluck it, fry it. The museum may also provide the answer to the eternal riddle: why did the chicken cross the road? In the light of the exhibits here, it was clearly to have its portrait painted.

ADDRESS: Habongam-dong 141-4, Dongducheon-si, Gyeonggi-do, 483-110 South Korea

TEL: +82 31 928 5899

OPEN: Daily, except Monday, 10 a.m.–6 p.m.

ADMISSION: 4,000 won (about £2.20) adults; 2,000 won (about £1.10) children.

THAILAND

TILLEKE & GIBBINS MUSEUM OF COUNTERFEIT GOODS, BANGKOK

Before you are tempted to buy that oh-so-cheap Rolex or bargain designer handbag from a Bangkok market stall, it might be worth paying a visit to the city's Museum of Counterfeit Goods. Thousands of counterfeit goods are seized in raids across Bangkok every day, and more than 4,000 dodgy items, including clothing, footwear, watches, sunglasses, mobile phones, perfume, cigarettes, alcohol, foodstuffs, car parts and electrical gadgets, are displayed as a warning to the public in the offices of law firm Tilleke & Gibbins on the twenty-sixth floor of the Supalai Grand Tower. The museum was established in 1989 by the firm's David Lyman, and what started off as a modest collection of around 100 items has since ballooned to feature all manner of infringing products accumulated by the firm in the course of its work.

The guided tours are conducted by Tilleke & Gibbins attorneys, who expose the myth that intellectual property infringement is a victimless crime. You will learn how fake products can often endanger the health of both those who buy them and those who produce them, how counterfeiting and piracy rob the government of tax revenue, and how they are frequently linked to other forms of organised crime, including drugs, firearms, human trafficking, and even terrorism. It may be easy to dismiss the seriousness of fake Lacoste T-shirts, but fake medication and fake car brake pads are no laughing matter. It is not only expensive goods that the counterfeiters target: the museum displays fake shampoo (in real shampoo bottles), fake toothpaste, fake ballpoint pens and even fake staples.

On a practical note, you will be taught how to spot fake goods, as the forgeries are put on display next to their genuine counterparts, to stop you returning home with a pirate version of *Pirates of the Caribbean* or a bargain *Downton Abbey* box set that has been dubbed into Russian. Scarily, you can also buy fake Pot Noodle in Bangkok, so watch out for that telltale Not Poodle label.

ADDRESS: 1011 Rama 3 Road, Supalai Grand Tower, Bangkok, Thailand

TEL: +66 2653 5555

WEBSITE: www.tilleke.com

OPEN: Monday, 2–3 p.m.; Thursday, 10–11 a.m. By appointment only. Book at least 24 hours in advance.

ADMISSION: Free

AUSTRALASIA

AUSTRALIA

MAD MAX 2 MUSEUM, SILVERTON, NEW SOUTH WALES

At the last count, Silverton, a small mining town in the desert outback 800 miles west of Sydney, had a population of around 35. Yet since 2010 it has also boasted a unique tourist attraction: a museum devoted to *Mad Max 2* put together by displaced Yorkshireman Adrian Bennett, a superfan who has seen the movie more than 200 times.

Reluctantly dragged along by his mates to see a double screening of *Mad Max* and its sequel in his native Bradford in 1982, Bennett underwent a life-changing experience. 'From the opening credits of *Mad Max* to the closing credits of *Mad Max 2: The Road Warrior*, my jaw was on the floor. They were the most unique, original films I had ever seen. Something grabbed hold of me during those films and I left the cinema a different person.' He became obsessed with finding every scrap of information he could about the films. His determination to visit the locations where they were shot eventually led him to up sticks and move his wife and children to Australia in 2006, first to Adelaide and three years later to Silverton, a major setting for *Mad Max 2*. He confessed: 'It got to the stage where I just had to live where *Mad Max 2* was filmed.'

It was not only his family he shipped to the other side of the world. A panel beater by trade, he had spent over £15,000 building a replica of Mad Max's Ford XB GT Interceptor car, so naturally that came, too.

Once in Australia, he began collecting whatever memorabilia he could lay his hands on: photographs, life-sized character models, props, costumes and more working vehicles, both originals and replicas. His prize possessions are the original boomerang and music box that the Feral Kid had in the movie, and he also likes to point out a replica of the nineteenth-century fork that Max used in the film to eat dog food. A replica fork? That really is an item for true fans only.

The locals, many of whom had been extras or stuntmen on *Mad Max* 2, welcomed him with open arms and willingly contributed items for the museum, a ramshackle-looking, post-apocalyptic-style shed attached to the Bennett family home. The location may be remote, but there is a steady stream of through traffic, and Mad Max fans have been making the pilgrimage to the area – known as the Hollywood of the Outback – for years. So maybe he wasn't that crazy for hauling his family 10,000 miles to set up a museum in the middle of nowhere paying homage to a movie sequel. Then again . . .

ADDRESS: 9 Sterling St., Silverton NSW 2880, Australia

TEL: + 61 8 8088 6128

EMAIL: madmaxmuseum@yahoo.com.au

WEBSITE: www.silverton.org.au/madmaxmuseum.html

OPEN: May–August, 9 a.m.–5 p.m.; September–April, 10 a.m.–4 p.m. (call or email in advance).

ADMISSION: AUD$7.50 (about £3.50)

MUSEUM OF HUMAN DISEASE, SYDNEY,
NEW SOUTH WALES

Established in the 1960s by Donald Wilhelm, Professor of Pathology at the University of New South Wales, the Museum of Human Disease was originally only open to medical experts and students, but now you too can get closer than you would probably wish to more than 3,000 diseases. It is rather like visiting a vast, old-fashioned sweet shop, but instead of humbugs, pear drops and aniseed balls, the individual jars contain human tissue infected with, for example, tuberculosis, gangrene, or cirrhosis of the liver. Each specimen has been obtained either from organs removed during surgery or at the autopsy of a patient who chose to donate their body to science, and because the tissue samples come from real people, each has its own background story, which is often revealed in all its gory detail.

'There is great suffering in every single jar,' notes the museum director, and it is hard not to agree when confronted with an inflamed appendix, a chronic peptic ulcer, a pulmonary embolism, a malignant brain tumour, an arthritic knee joint affected by gout, and an amputated foot with blackened, gangrenous toes. Arguably the most disturbing item is the benign teratoma of an ovary, which has teeth and hair growing from it. Some specimens date back more than 100 years and are from diseases that thankfully have largely been eradicated by modern medicine. Diphtheria and typhoid are now rare in Australia, and as such their specimens are virtually irreplaceable.

By providing this arduous tour of infectious and non-infectious diseases past and present, the museum hopes to educate people about lifestyle. To this end, there are separate exhibits on smoking, obesity, drugs and alcohol. If you need a reason to quit smoking, consider the case of a thirty-three-year-old man who puffed twenty cigarettes a day, was overweight and had a history of high blood pressure. His poor heart, which suffered three heart attacks in five weeks (the last one fatal), is displayed in five slices to show the full range of the blood clot and dead muscle.

The museum proudly boasts that its collection contains almost 99 per cent of all causes of death in modern Australia. Basically, whatever is going to kill you can be found here. So if you're someone who faints at the sight of a needle or a drop of blood, you might be advised to stick to the beach or the Opera House.

ADDRESS: Ground Floor, Samuels Building, UNSW Sydney NSW 2052

TEL: +61 2 9385 1522

EMAIL: diseasemuseum@unsw.edu.au

WEBSITE: www.diseasemuseum.unsw.edu.au

OPEN: Monday–Friday, 10 a.m.–4 p.m.

ADMISSION: AUD$10 (£4.80) adults; AUD$5 (£2.40) children.

OLD UMBRELLA SHOP AND MUSEUM, LAUNCESTON, TASMANIA

Although Hobart is Australia's second driest state capital, the city of Launceston on the northern side of Tasmania is no stranger to rainfall, making an umbrella an essential item for any household. The go-to place for keeping dry in Launceston is the heritage-listed Old Umbrella Shop, an establishment that has changed little in appearance since the 1900s. It still has many of the old fixtures and fittings (including the original till), although sadly the prices it rings up are all too modern.

Down the decades it was operated by three generations of the Shott family, who made and repaired umbrellas, in later years also handcrafting various wood souvenirs on the premises from native timbers. The shop's founder, Robert Walter Shott, pioneered the promotion of a steel rib umbrella frame by British industrialist Samuel Fox, which proved far more practical than the previous frames made from whalebone. Shott also presented a walking stick to the then Prince of Wales (the future Edward VIII) when he visited Tasmania in 1920. The family business was held in such high esteem that every civic visitor to Launceston after the Second World War was presented with a handmade wood souvenir from Shott & Son.

As well as selling bright, shiny new umbrellas, the shop is now home to a small National Trust-run museum of vintage umbrellas housed in original blackwood display cases. Some of the items on show date back more than 100 years, which is a testament to their sturdiness considering that some of today's lightweight umbrellas sustain irreparable rib damage at the first puff of wind. The museum also chronicles the Shott family's passion for umbrellas. It is almost enough to make you hope for rain when you step outside.

ADDRESS: 60 George Street, Launceston TAS 7250, Australia

TEL: +61 3 6331 9248

WEBSITE: wwww.nationaltrust.org.au/places/
old-umbrella-shop/

OPEN: Monday–Friday, 9 a.m.–5 p.m.; Saturday
9 a.m.-noon.

ADMISSION: Free

NEW ZEALAND

NEW ZEALAND BEER CAN MUSEUM, GALATEA, NORTH ISLAND

You might expect a museum on a dairy farm to be devoted to milk bottles, but Barry Steiner's is dedicated to beer cans – more than 12,000 of them. The man with the appropriate surname for a connoisseur of beer receptacles started his collection in 1987 at the age of twelve, when he found a couple of discarded beer cans by the roadside on his way home from school. He began scouring rubbish bins and dumps for further examples, and now travels the world adding to his collection, which features beer cans from over 160 countries. He keeps them neatly arranged on shelves in a large shed on his farm, and has an encyclopaedic knowledge about each can. His prize possessions include a set of special 007 cans featuring pictures of the first seven Bond girls, and a 1935 American can, one of the first pair to be produced commercially. This historic can was sold by the Gottfried Krueger Brewery in Richmond, Virginia, and is now worth around NZD$10,000 (£4,300). The American Can Co. had tried experimenting with canned beer as early as 1909, but abandoned the idea because their cans were unable to withstand the pressure from carbonation and kept exploding, a trait unlikely to appeal to customers.

As well as cans, Barry, who even has a beer-can telephone, displays other beer-related paraphernalia such as signs, coasters and trays, plus a collection of vintage farm tractors and classic cars. He also keeps another 1,000 beer cans in his house. Since leaving the beer can full adds no value to the item, Barry has personally drunk the contents of many in his collection, although ironically he reckons that beer tastes better from a glass.

For a small fee, visitors receive not only a guided tour of the museum but also a free drink.

ADDRESS:	374 Jolly Road, Galatea, Rotorua, Bay of Plenty 3272, New Zealand
TEL:	+ 64 7 366 4039
EMAIL:	barrygalateasteiner@msn.com
OPEN:	By appointment.
ADMISSION:	NZD$5 (£2.25)

SOCK WORLD AND SOCK-KNITTING MACHINE
MUSEUM, HOKITIKA, SOUTH ISLAND

One commodity that is not in short supply in New Zealand is wool. Therefore it made sense that during both world wars the country's womenfolk formed community groups to knit socks for soldiers. Knitting manually, they were hard pressed to manage more than a sock each per day, so many bought hand-cranked sock-knitting machines to speed up the production process. The idea was that a company would sell the women the machines and then buy back the finished socks, although in times of peace, when there was less demand, the unscrupulous sock machine companies often reneged on the deal, leaving these women with piles of unwanted socks. On the plus side, they never again had to worry about what to get their husbands for birthdays and Christmas.

Notwithstanding the sharp business practice, these old machines played an important part in New Zealand history. Dairy farmer Jacquie Grant used to spin wool on long winter evenings and, not being a hand-knitter, was delighted when presented with an old circular sock-knitting machine that had been rusting in a shed. She restored it, began making socks and then set about tracking down other sock machines that had seen better days. She has now assembled the world's largest display of fully-restored vintage sock machines known to man, some capable of knocking out ten pairs in an hour. Over 200 are on show at her museum, from Britain, the United States, Canada, France and, of course, New Zealand. The majority are hand-cranked machines designed for use by housewives, but there are also larger industrial models. So stand and marvel at such delights as the Green Harmony Autoknitter from Maine, the British Bulldog, the English Beehive, and the incomparable 1880 Griswold – all while watching a compelling video on the history of sock making.

The machine museum is part of Sock World, which declares itself to be the 'world's greatest sock store'. So after perusing the vintage contraptions, you can treat yourself to a pair of hand-cranked socks in a huge variety of yarns, including possum and merino. Socks will never seem the same again.

ADDRESS: 27 Sewell Street, Hokitika 7810, New Zealand

TEL: +64 3 755 7251

WEBSITE: www.autoknitter.com

OPEN: Daily, 9 a.m.–5 p.m.

ADMISSION: Free

SOUTH AMERICA

PERU

BRAIN MUSEUM, LIMA

As the English translation suggests, the *Museo de Cerebros* is all about human brains, but not just any brains – diseased and damaged brains. Run by neuropathologist Diana Rivas, the museum has been collecting brains and neurologically deformed foetuses since 1947, and now has more than 3,000 examples, showing abnormalities caused by disease, substance abuse damage, injuries and psychological disorder.

Although the Harvard Brain Tissue Resource Center at McLean Hospital in Massachusetts has around 7,000 specimens, its brains aren't open to the public, making the Lima museum, which is part of Peru's Institute of Neurological Science, a unique display. It is certainly not somewhere for the timid or squeamish. Indeed, museum staff expect to deal with at least a couple of cases of fainting visitors every month.

Some 300 brains are on permanent display, housed in jars filled with formaldehyde. Among various brains that have been damaged by AIDS, Alzheimer's, Parkinson's disease, aneuryisms, heart attacks, haemorrhages, alcoholism, drug abuse, strokes and tumours, there is a rare victim of Creutzfeldt-Jacob disease, better known as the human strain of mad cow disease. This is Dr Rivas's favourite specimen. When medical students dissected it, they had to cover the laboratory with plastic sheeting and wear protective 'astronaut' clothing to handle the brain, even though it had been in formaldehyde for a month. 'The prion proteins that cause the disease are microscopic and extremely resilient,' Rivas explained. 'Everybody is afraid of that one.'

Jars also contain examples of brains damaged by parasitic roundworms after people have eaten undercooked meat (usually pork) – a common occurrence in Peru. The hope is that, by seeing the damage certain lifestyles and diets can do to a human brain, visitors will mend their ways in future.

The museum also contains an autopsy room where Dr Rivas supervises 100 autopsies a year, giving her a first look at potential new exhibits. 'For me, cutting brains is like peeling potatoes,' she says matter-of-factly. If she uses the same knife for both tasks, let's hope she remembers to rinse it first.

ADDRESS: Instituto Nacional de Ciencias Neurologicas, Jr. Ancash 1271, Ancon, Lima, Peru

TEL: +51 1 411 7768

EMAIL: patologiaiecn@icn.minsa.gob.pe

WEBSITE: www.icn.minsa.gob.pe/index.php/museo

OPEN: Monday–Saturday, 8 a.m.–12.30 p.m.

ADMISSION: S/15.00 (about £3) for foreign nationals.

URUGUAY

ANDES TRAGEDY AND MIRACLE (1972) MUSEUM, MONTEVIDEO

On Friday 13 October 1972, a Uruguayan airplane en route from Montevideo to Santiago, Chile, carrying a team of high school rugby players along with their friends and relatives, crashed 13,000 feet up in the Andes. Of the 45 passengers and crew members on board, 32 initially survived, but many had sustained serious injuries, and with hardly any provisions – just a few sweets, some cans of food and a couple of bottles of alcohol – and freezing temperatures, their chances of pulling through were slim. For ten long days and nights they waited to be rescued, and then they heard on their pocket radio that the search for them had been called off.

Worse was to come on the night of day 16, when a devastating avalanche hit them while they were sleeping in the remains of the fuselage, burying them in snow and killing another eight people. In order to survive, they drank water made from snow and, rather more controversially, ate the flesh of their dead companions. Eventually two of the group felt strong enough to make a bid for freedom from the 'Valley of Tears'. They hiked for ten days until they came across a cattle drover, who in turn rode for eight hours to the nearest police station to summon help.

Finally, after 72 days trapped on the mountain, the ordeal of the 16 who were still alive was over. All that remained was to explain to a disbelieving world precisely how they had managed to survive for so long without food.

The remarkable story of the passengers so desperate they were forced to resort to cannibalism was told in the 1993 movie *Alive*, based on the book by Piers Paul Read, and is again now at the recently opened *Museo Andes 1972*, a private venture set up by the Uruguayan businessman Jörg Thomsen to honour the 29 who perished and the 16 who came back from the dead. Their miraculous tale of survival is related by means of photographs, video, documents, newspaper articles, interviews with survivors, personal belongings, clothing and pieces of airplane debris that you are actually allowed to touch. A timeline puts the crash in historical context, so that visitors can see that, while the rest of the world was coming to terms with the re-election of Richard Nixon and the release of the latest Wings single, these people were eating the bodies of their friends just to survive. As the title of the museum suggests, the narrative leans towards the inspirational rather than the gruesome, although naturally the C-word is on everyone's lips. The most fascinating items are letters written by two ill-fated passengers – one who later died in the avalanche, the other who succumbed to his injuries after waiting to be rescued for over a month. Though the museum is relatively small, the artefacts are so moving and the story so compelling that you will find yourself spending at least an hour there. It also helps that there is an English translation.

ADDRESS: Rincón 619, Ciudad Vieja, Montevideo 11000, Uruguay

Tel: +598 2916 9461

Website: www.mandes.uy

Open: Monday–Friday, 10 a.m.–5 p.m.; Saturday, 10 a.m.–3 p.m.

Admission: 200 pesos (about £4.50)

NORTH AMERICA

CANADA

GOPHER HOLE MUSEUM, TORRINGTON, ALBERTA

There are not many places in the world where you can go and see a dead gopher in a bikini, but Torrington, Alberta, is one. In fact, at the Gopher Hole Museum you can see stuffed gophers dressed in tiny costumes in dozens of different guises – as fishermen, firefighters, native Americans, a hairdresser, a pastor and even a bank robber – in around fifty enchanting dioramas depicting the history and daily life of the small Canadian town.

Back in 1996 not only was the local economy in dire need of a boost, but Torrington was also being overrun by wild gophers. So some bright spark came up with the idea of killing two birds (or more accurately seventy gophers) with one stone, by having the rodents slaughtered, stuffed by a taxidermist and then placed in miniature scenes featuring them in anthropomorphic poses. The imaginative settings include a library, the local bar (complete with pool table), a hunting expedition, a playground, a hairdressing salon, a market and a wedding ceremony. And if you wondered why the service at the Torrington Post Office is so slow, it is because the worker behind the counter is a gopher, and a lifeless one at that. Many of the tableaux have witty captions, such as a domestic post-dinner scene where one gopher says to the other, 'Oh boy, am I ever stuffed!'

With around 6,000 visitors to the museum a year, Torrington has sought to make itself the go-to gopher destination. Fire hydrants in the town are painted as gophers, and a 14-foot-high gopher statue welcomes visitors to Torrington. Even so, the museum has attracted a measure of controversy, with animal rights campaigners protesting about the killings. The museum counters that crop-eating gophers are a real problem for local farmers. 'We have to kill them,' explained one worker. 'Is it so bad to put them on display afterwards?' Whatever the rights and wrongs, the resultant publicity helped put Torrington and its quirky little gopher museum on the world map.

ADDRESS: 208 1st Street South, Torrington, AB T0M 2B0, Canada

TEL: +1 403 631 2133

WEBSITE: gopherholemuseum.ca

OPEN: Daily, 1 June–30 September, 10 a.m.–5 p.m.

ADMISSION: $2

TREKCETERA MUSEUM, VULCAN, ALBERTA

The small town of Vulcan was originally named in the early twentieth century by a Canadian Pacific Railway surveyor after the Roman god of fire, but it was in the late 1960s that it really hit the jackpot, when Leonard Nimoy's supremely logical, half-Vulcan, half-human Spock tried to bring a little order to *Star Trek*. Capitalising on the happy coincidence, the town eventually built a *Star Trek*-themed tourist station, installed space-themed murals and signs, exhibited a replica of the starship *Enterprise* from *Star Trek* V, commissioned a bust of Nimoy (unveiled in 2010 by the actor himself), hosted an annual Trekkie convention called 'Spock Days', and struck a deal with CBS to become the world's first officially licensed *Star Trek* destination. There was no chance of anyone leaving Vulcan without knowing of its connection to Captain Kirk and co. To reinforce the link still further, in 2013 the Trekcetera museum was opened to mark the town's centenary.

Proudly proclaiming itself as Canada's only *Star Trek* museum and dedicated to *Star Trek* creator Gene Roddenberry, it features original props, costumes and pre-production items from the TV series and the films, including the one-of-a-kind, 460-pound command chair from the set of Paramount's 2002 movie *Star Trek: Nemesis*. Curator Michael Mangold acts as an enthusiastic and knowledgeable guide, so even if you're not a dyed-in-the-wool Trekkie with a lifelong ambition to see a Klingon dress in close-up, it might be worth boldly going inside.

Curiously, the museum also displays some non-*Star Trek* items, including props and costumes from *Thunderbirds*, *Superman*, *Brokeback Mountain*, the Harry Potter movies and *Titanic*. Meanwhile, in the gift shop you can buy the original soap (well, by the same manufacturer) that was used in First Class on board

Titanic on its maiden – and only – voyage, and even the very brand of tea that was supplied to the workers who built *Titanic*. Don't expect the soap to float in the bath.

ADDRESS:	118 2nd Avenue South, Vulcan, AB T0L 2B0, Canada
TEL:	+1 403 485 6611
WEBSITE:	www.trekcetera.com
OPEN:	Daily, 10 a.m.–5 p.m.
ADMISSION:	$12, adults; $9, seniors; $8, children 7–17 years; free, children 6 and under, if accompanied by adult.

MEXICO

CANCÚN UNDERWATER MUSEUM, CANCÚN

Tourists often visit museums to keep out of the rain, but at this museum you are almost guaranteed to get wet, because the whole thing is underwater. Although you can see the exhibits through the crystal-clear water from the dry comfort of a glass-bottomed boat, the best way to appreciate the 500 sculptures submerged in up to 25 feet of water off the coast at Cancún is to go snorkelling or scuba diving.

The *Museo Subacuático de Arte* (MUSA) was conceived in 2008 by Cancún National Marine Park director Jaime Gonzalez Canto and sculptor Jason deCaires Taylor, with the intention that the sculptures would eventually be transformed by nature into a coral reef that would attract marine life, thereby replenishing some of the natural reefs that have been damaged over the years by the influx of visitors. Taylor, a qualified diving instructor, is one of six sculptors whose work is exhibited. His installation *Silent Evolution* depicts members of a local fishing community, Puerto Morelos, and required 120 tons of concrete, sand and gravel. The statues had to be lowered into place by a forty-ton crane before being fixed to the seabed. Another of his sculptures, The Banker, features men in suits literally burying their heads in the sand. As well as the human figures, there is a submerged sculpture of a full-sized

VW Beetle fitted out as a 'lobster hotel', with openings for the shellfish to enter and shelves for them to seek refuge inside. The total installations cover an area of over 4,500 square feet.

The three-hour tour by Aquaworld involves a boat trip to and from the artificial reef, where you can scuba dive or snorkel for forty-five minutes around the museum amidst schools of fish, turtles and rays. If the weather is favourable, the boat will take you to a second site in shallower water, which is rich in marine life and where you can snorkel – but not scuba dive – for a further twenty minutes. Other dive operators are available, and naturally once you express an interest in undertaking a tour of the museum, you will be flooded with tempting offers.

A life vest must be worn when snorkelling, and a local guide must be used when diving. If you want to scuba dive, you must be in possession of an official diving certificate. If you need to obtain one there, it will cost you more.

ADDRESS: Marina, Cancún, Quintana Roo, Mexico

TEL: +52 998 887 5501: Aquaworld +52 998 848 8326/7

WEBSITE: musacancun.org

OPEN: Daily, 7 a.m.–8 p.m.

ADMISSION: Prices vary according to dive operator. Average for diving/snorkelling: $45 adults; $25 children 8–11 years.

USA

HAMMER MUSEUM, HAINES, ALASKA

It is a remarkable fact that Man has so far created more than 2,000 different types of hammer in the course of his existence, but even more remarkable that a museum has been opened to celebrate that fact. Haines bills itself as the 'Adventure Capital of Alaska', with snowmobile racing, kayaking, rafting, jet-ski rides and, since 2002, the world's only museum devoted entirely to hammers.

The man responsible for this hammerfest is Dave Pahl, who moved from Cleveland, Ohio, to Alaska in 1973 because he wanted to earn a living with his bare hands. To that end, he became a self-taught blacksmith, and began collecting hammers old and new, receiving some as gifts and acquiring others on specific 'hammer hunting' expeditions. While most people might be tempted to keep such a collection to themselves, Dave thought it merited being seen by a wider audience, and so he and his wife Carol opened up the Hammer Museum in a century-old building in Haines. 'When I told people I was doing a hammer museum, I got ridiculed a little bit,' said Dave. 'But when I was digging the foundation, I found this 800-year-old Tlingit hammer, and I took it as a good omen.'

He has hammers from ancient Rome right through the indus-trial period and up to the present day. As well as traditional hammers used in mining, carpentry and car repairs, the museum houses hammers used by bankers, barristers, cobblers, doctors, dentists, musicians and even by nightclub goers in the 1920s and 1930s to applaud the band. There are glass hammers, two-handled hammers and a hammer made of ball bearings, and Dave is proud to say that he has over fifty hammer patents on display. The building is easily recognisable by the twenty-foot-tall hammer that stands in front.

The museum states that its mission is 'to research, identify, exhibit and preserve the history of hammers for the education of the general public.' Most of the novelty hammers were picked up by Carol Pahl, who wanted to attract a broader range of visitors, and not just blokes who like whacking things with big hammers. Her strategy seems to have paid off as, despite its relatively remote location, the museum attracts a steady flow of people in the summer months. One satisfied customer hit the nail on the head when he said that the experience gave him 'a new-found appreciation for hammers.' Praise does not come much higher than that.

ADDRESS:	108 Main Street, Haines, AK 99827, USA
TEL:	+1 907 766 2374
WEBSITE:	www.thehammermuseum.org
OPEN:	May–September, Monday–Friday, 10 a.m.–5 p.m.; July only, also Saturday, 10 a.m.–2 p.m.
ADMISSION:	$5 adults. Children 12 and under free when accompanied by an adult.

WORLD'S SMALLEST MUSEUM, SUPERIOR, ARIZONA

To lure customers to their Buckboard City Café next door, in 1996 Dan Wight and Jake Reaney stuffed a shed boasting a floor space of just 134 square feet with some of their personal belongings and called it the World's Smallest Museum. Although it can no longer claim that title (as anyone who has stepped inside a Welsh telephone kiosk will testify), this is a proper little museum, with exhibits divided into ten different sections and displayed behind glass panels. It is more than just a dumping ground for bits of accumulated tat; it represents artefacts spanning over a century of American history, covering areas from pop culture to the Wild West, from politics to the kitchen.

The star attraction is the world's largest Apache tear (a good-luck stone), but that is not the only record holder on display, as the World's Smallest Museum proudly presents the world's largest fake Zippo lighter. Visitors will also stumble across such diverse items as an old photograph of Oprah Winfrey when she was still an ambitious young news reporter in Tennessee, the last photograph of Apache leader and medicine man Geronimo, a nineteenth-century frying pan, a 1917 typewriter, a 1984 Compaq computer (with 10MB hard drive), an old coal-fired iron, a 1920s miner's lunch box, a 1950s popcorn popper, barbed wire from a Second World War Japanese internment camp in Arizona, an early Beatles poster, and a 1960 letter to Reaney from President-elect John F. Kennedy. There is also a memorial to Wyatt Earp's second wife, Mattie Blaylock, who is buried a couple of miles away. One visitor neatly described the place as a 'combination of kitsch, cleverness and benign neglect.'

'It's all about ordinary life,' says Dan Wight. 'You'll hear people say, "Yeah, I had one of those." It brings back memories for everybody.' Some people look around the place in only three minutes; others linger for half an hour.

Dan and Jake clearly don't believe in throwing stuff out. What doesn't fit into the museum goes on the roof or is incorporated into curious sculptures. Thus part of the museum roof is made from 1,800 reused aluminium beer cans, while outside is a series of fountains and waterfalls constructed from recycled junk, notably large tyres. The World's Smallest Museum is big on imagination.

ADDRESS:	1111 West Highway 60, Superior, AZ 85173, USA
TEL:	+1 520 208 0634 (museum) or +1 520 689 5800 (café)
OPEN:	Wednesday–Sunday, 8 a.m.–1.30 p.m. Times may vary, so call in advance.
ADMISSION:	Free

CHAFFEE BARBERSHOP MUSEUM, FORT SMITH, ARKANSAS

On 20 December 1957, twenty-two-year-old Elvis Presley, far and away the biggest rock 'n' roll star in the world, received his draft notice to join the US Army. Whereas many of his teenage fans openly wept, Elvis accepted the news stoically. 'It's a duty I've got to fill and I'm going to do it,' he said. He was initially ordered to report for duty the following month, but received a deferment because he was filming his fourth movie, *King Creole.* So it was not until 24 March 1958 that he was finally inducted, and the next day he sat down in Building 803 at Fort Chaffee, Arkansas, to have his head shaved. He was given the obligatory GI buzz cut by barber James Petersen in a room packed with reporters and photographers. One local newspaper snapper, Jack Cleavenger, asked Presley to blow his freshly cut hair out of his hand. The ever-courteous 'King' obliged, and Cleavenger sent off the picture with the caption, 'Hair Today, Gone Tomorrow'. The shearing of Elvis's locks was so newsworthy it was described as the haircut that was 'heard around the world'.

Even though Elvis only spent a few days at Chaffee, the fort barbershop, as with all things related to him, became something of a shrine, attracting worldwide interest. Decades later, a local school decided it was history that needed to be preserved, and raised enough money for the building to be opened up as a proper museum, making it the only museum in the world dedicated to a single haircut.

Restored to exactly how it looked on that fateful day in 1958 with authentic period items (including what is claimed to be the very chair on which Elvis sat while having his hair cut), the Chaffee Barbershop Museum opened its doors to the public in 2008. Rare photos from Presley's short stay in the area are displayed, along with an emotional letter sent by three teenage girls to President Eisenhower in which they said they would 'just die' if the Army cut off Elvis's sideburns. It did and they didn't. Other artefacts document the seventy-year history of Fort Chaffee, which in its time has housed German prisoners of war, Cuban refugees, relocated Vietnamese citizens and New Orleans residents displaced by Hurricane Katrina. There is also memorabilia from some of the movies filmed at the base, including *Biloxi Blues* (with Matthew Broderick), *The Tuskegee Airmen* and *A Soldier's Story*.

Every year around 25 March fans descend on the museum for an Elvis Haircut Day celebration, when they can receive a buzz cut by James Petersen's son, Jimmy Don Petersen, who is also a barber, which is a blessing for all concerned. Jimmy Don was around nine years old when his father cut Elvis's hair, but understandably at the time he did not appreciate the significance of the event. 'He asked me to go down there to watch the haircut, but I told him I wanted to stay home and play with my friends. I look back and I really regret it.' Visitors also get the chance to have their photo taken in the chair with a cardboard cut-out of Elvis, an offer few can apparently resist. Elvis may have left the building, but his haircut remains.

ADDRESS: 7313 Terry Street, Fort Smith, AR 72923, USA

TEL: +1 479 452 4554

WEBSITE: chaffeecrossing.com

OPEN: Monday–Saturday, 9 a.m.–4 p.m., except national holidays.

ADMISSION: Free

BIGFOOT DISCOVERY PROJECT AND MUSEUM, FELTON, CALIFORNIA

Michael Rugg is in little doubt that any day, month or year soon the existence of Bigfoot will be confirmed. Cynics might scoff that the elusive Sasquatch could be hiding out in the woods with Lord Lucan, Shergar and the crew of the *Mary Celeste*, but, be honest, how many people believed in the existence of Boris Johnson until a few years ago?

Rugg has been fascinated with Bigfoot and its equally hairy Himalayan cousin the Yeti since he was a small boy. He began collecting newspaper articles, photographs, books and other arte-facts in the 1950s, keeping them at his Felton home in the Santa Cruz Mountains of northern California, a rumoured Bigfoot hotspot. As a student in 1967, he wrote a paper for an anthropol-ogy class that featured a map highlighting Bluff Creek, California, as the ideal place to spot one of the mysterious primates. Seven months later, Roger Patterson and Bob Gimlin shot a film purporting to show a female Pacific Coast Sasquatch – nicknamed 'Patty' – walking upright on two legs at that very location. Rugg went on to carve a career first in the folk music business and then in computer graphics, but he never lost his obsession with Bigfoot, cryptozoology or the paranormal in general, and in 2004 he and his partner, Paula Yarr, opened the Bigfoot Discovery Project and Museum with a view to sharing their knowledge and evidence and perhaps even winning over a few of the non-believers.

Apart from the gift shop selling various mugs, stickers and T-shirts, most of the exhibits in the small cabin that houses the museum are linked to suspected local sightings of Bigfoot. A map marked with coloured pins shows the location of each reported encounter in Santa Cruz County. There are plaster foot and hand prints from something big, a plaster cast of 'Sasquatch faeces', what may or may not be a Bigfoot tooth, audio tapes of an alleged Bigfoot scream, and Rugg's collection of memorabilia. These include a sensational tabloid newspaper story by a woman with a hairy child beneath the headline: I HAD BIGFOOT'S BABY. However, the most intriguing item is the Patterson-Gimlin film, which is shown on a continuous loop and which Rugg considers to be definitive proof of the existence of Bigfoot. Is it simply a man in an ape suit? Both filmmakers steadfastly denied that the footage was a hoax.

Rugg himself claims to have seen Bigfoot twice with his own eyes, the first occasion when he was just four. He is convinced that the discovery of Bigfoot is just around the corner – or maybe behind that tree. 'We have a number of eye witnesses who have reported sightings,' he says. 'We've come up with more evidence to indicate it's true than the opposite.' If Bigfoot does finally decide to go public, let's hope it repays Michael Rugg's faith by volunteering to do a stint behind the counter at the museum, provided they can find a T-shirt to fit it.

ADDRESS: 5497 Highway 9, Felton, CA 95018, USA

TEL: +1 831 335 4478

WEBSITE: bigfootdiscoveryproject.com

OPEN: Wednesday–Monday (11 a.m.–6 p.m.).
Closed Tuesday.

ADMISSION: Free (Donations accepted)

BUNNY MUSEUM, PASADENA, CALIFORNIA

When Steve Lubanski gave his then girlfriend Candace Frazee a stuffed rabbit as a Valentine's Day gift in 1993 because she had called him her 'Honey Bunny', it started a tradition of each presenting the other with a new bunny gift on a daily basis. These romantic gestures eventually led to marriage, and a record-breaking obsession that resulted in the couple filling their home with more than 31,000 items of rabbit-related memorabilia.

Their house has been turned into a rabbit museum – 'the hoppiest place in the world' – crammed from floor to ceiling with stuffed bunnies, ceramic bunnies and bunnies in the form of cookie jars, furniture, light fittings, fridge magnets, toiletries, books and games. Candace, who wears bunny earrings, cleans her teeth with a bunny toothbrush and washes with a rabbit-shaped bar of soap, is only too happy to share her collection with the public. 'We are filling a need we didn't even know existed,' she said in an interview. 'People own a Renoir or a Matisse, and they're the only ones who see it. That's selfish. People should share what they have.'

While an 'Elvis Parsley' water jug is the most popular item with visitors, some of the artefacts are genuine antiques. There is a rabbit ring that dates back to around the third century BC, an 1,800-year-old bunny brooch, and a bunny gunpowder flask from the American Civil War. Another oddity is the rabbit figurine carved from volcanic ash that spewed out of Mount St Helens in 1980. The strangest pieces in the museum, however, are undoubtedly the freeze-dried rabbits, which were once real household pets but, upon death, have been preserved in a glass display case. Touchingly, Candace presented Steve with one to celebrate their nineteenth wedding anniversary in 2013. The rabbit may have been dead, but the romance clearly wasn't. Steve could hardly have been surprised – after all, this is a man who dressed in a white rabbit costume at his own reception. Naturally the wedding cake that day was carrot cake. Luckily for Steve, Candace is no bunny boiler. In fact, she is vegetarian, so there is no danger of any of her collection ending up on the menu.

It would seem that even stuffed rabbits multiply at an alarming rate, and they have now outgrown their home, forcing Candace and Steve to consider moving them to larger premises elsewhere in Pasadena. Until then, you can't miss their house: it's the one with the giant rabbit topiary on the front lawn.

ADDRESS: 1933 Jefferson Drive, Pasadena, CA 91104, USA

TEL: +1 626 798 8848

WEBSITE: www.thebunnymuseum.com

OPEN: By appointment.

ADMISSION: $5 donation suggested. Children under 4 free.

BURLINGAME MUSEUM OF PEZ MEMORABILIA, BURLINGAME, CALIFORNIA

First marketed in 1927 to help adults who wanted to quit smoking, Pez is a brand of Austrian candy that has gone on to become hugely popular in the United States, as much for the ever-changing designs of the Pez dispensers as for the sweets themselves. When Pez originally came to the US in 1952, the product was sold in tins and struggled to make any impact, but then, in a stroke of genius, the company switched to dispensers, put cute heads on the tops and targeted children as their chief market. These dispensers have graduated to the status of collectibles, selling for up to $7,000 apiece, the high prices even creating a lucrative line in fake Pez dispensers.

The museum was opened in 1995 by avid Pez dispenser collectors Gary and Nancy Doss, who ran a computer repair shop at the time, and hoped that the dispenser display might prove a pleasant diversion for customers. It quickly became apparent, however, that visitors were more interested in the dispensers than the computers, which were subsequently squeezed out. The Burlingame Museum of Pez Memorabilia, as it was re-named, contains an example of every Pez dispenser ever sold – more than 1,000 in total, ranging from Disney favourites, *Angry Birds* and *Teenage Mutant Ninja Turtles* to Mozart, Mary Poppins and characters from *Lord of the Rings* and *Pirates of the Caribbean*. This must be the only place in the world where Barbie meets Kung Fu Panda –surely a movie waiting to be made. There is also the world's largest Pez dispensing machine, standing an impressive 7 feet 10 inches tall.

One item never on display is the infamous Hitler Pez dispenser. The pocket Führer was sold by mail order until Pez company lawyers stepped in and shut down the counterfeit operation. There are reckoned to be around fifty Pez Hitlers still in existence, making it much sought-after despite its bootleg status.

You actually get three museums for the price of one here, because within the main museum can also be found the Classic Toy Museum and the Banned Toy Museum, a small collection of toys taken off the market because they were either a serious safety hazard or considered offensive. They include Spanish Barbie, whose Matador costume prompted animal-loving Barbie fans led by actress Alicia Silverstone to write to Mattel asking the company to discontinue the doll; *Air Pirates*, a 1971 comic that portrayed Disney characters engaging in what can only be described as explicit behaviour; and the 1951 Atomic Energy Laboratory set, which, perhaps unwisely for a children's plaything, used real radioactive materials. Ah, the warm glow of childhood.

ADDRESS: 214 California Drive, Burlingame, CA 94010, USA
TEL: +1 650 347 2301
WEBSITE: www.burlingamepezmuseum.com
OPEN: Tuesday–Saturday, 10.30 a.m.–5.30 p.m.
ADMISSION: $3 adults; $2 children 4–10 years.

GOOD VIBRATIONS ANTIQUE VIBRATOR MUSEUM, SAN FRANCISCO, CALIFORNIA

When Joani Blank published her first edition of *Good Vibrations: The Complete Guide to Vibrators* in 1976, it created a real buzz. Responding to the vibes, customers at the Good Vibrations sex store she had founded in San Francisco began donating antique models they had picked up at flea markets or stumbled across during house clearances. Some had even inherited them. Who wants to be left a gold ring by your late grandmother when you can wear her Edwardian vibrator with pride? As the collection of antique vibrators grew, in 2012 it was decided to showcase them in a museum at the back of the store. Today the museum displays dozens of vibrators dating from the 1800s up to the 1970s. Quite apart from the titillation factor, the collection offers a fascinating insight into old medical practices.

In the Victorian era, medically induced orgasms were used by doctors as a cure for what was then labelled 'female hysteria', a wide-ranging condition characterised by symptoms such as anxiety, insomnia, irritability, loss of appetite and wanton lust. Single women would go to their doctor who, long before the digital age, proceeded to induce orgasm in the patient manually. It was a tough job, but someone had to do it. Help was at hand from 1869 with American doctor George Taylor's invention of the Manipulator, a steam-powered, coal-fired massager specifically designed to treat female disorders. British physician Joseph Mortimer Granville followed this with a cheaper, more portable, battery-operated model, and by the start of the twentieth century the new electric vibrator became widely available to the discerning medical professional. Soon the vibrator was being marketed in women's magazines for domestic use, often euphemistically described as a 'personal masseur' or 'magic wand'. It was always promoted as a health aid, giving a glowing complexion and shiny hair rather than any sexual benefits, although advertisers' claims that their product 'makes you fairly tingle with the joy of living' and that 'all the pleasure of youth will throb within you' left little to the imagination. So when vibrators began to appear in erotic films of the 1920s, magazines banned advertisements for them for fear of violating obscenity laws. The medical profession abandoned them, too, and they remained underground until the 1950s, when they resurfaced as 'massagers' marketed for weight loss. Even in the sexually liberated 1960s vibrators were sold primarily as beauty aids, not finally being acknowledged as sex toys until the following decade.

The early items on display at the museum bear little resemblance to the perky pink dildos of today. Some look more like food mixers or hairdryers. Before the battery-operated or electric vibrator, most models were operated by a hand-crank mechanism, which meant that instead of lying back and thinking of England, the user was more likely to be thinking of drilling a hole in a wall. Alarmingly, the Andis vibrator of 1933 was recommended for use by women and men, but purely as a scalp massager, while the Rolling Pin Heat Massager – a combination of vibrator and heated rolling pin from the same period – probably explained why grandma always had a smile on her face when she had baked a cake. The museum's curator, sexologist Carol Queen, says her most amazing find was a pneumatic vibrator that runs on compressed gas. 'You hooked it up to the kind of tank you see powering a pneumatic drill during street construction. Obviously, this is a device that didn't really catch on.'

The museum also features a collection of modern vibrators encrusted with jewels or artfully decorated. Although these are not for sale, you can always climax your visit by examining the multitude of eye-watering items on offer in the Good Vibrations shop.

ADDRESS: 1620 Polk Street, San Francisco, CA 94109, USA

TEL: +1 415 345 0400

EMAIL: antiques@goodvibes.com

WEBSITE: antiquevibratormuseum.com

OPEN: Daily, 12.30–6.30 p.m. Thursday, 12.30–8.30 p.m.

ADMISSION: Free

INTERNATIONAL BANANA MUSEUM, MECCA, CALIFORNIA

When it comes to simulated fruit artefacts, the one design shape that outstrips the rest is the banana. Thus the grandly titled, one-room International Banana Museum is home to over 20,000 banana-related items, ranging from telephones and lamps, knives and slippers to an eight-foot-long banana couch. Within these walls can also be found pepper shakers, hangers, staplers, compasses, candles, harmonicas, cookie jars, water guns, pipes, pencil sharpeners, inflatables, and even a record player shaped like a banana. There is also the world's only petrified banana. Well, it certainly doesn't look very relaxed.

The idea was the brainchild of Ken Bannister, the president of a photographic equipment manufacturing company. Back in the early 1970s, he handed out banana stickers at a manufacturers' conference as a joke, reasoning that if anything could put a smile on people's faces, it would be the fruit that is shaped like one. The reaction was so positive that he founded the International Banana Club, thereby becoming Top Banana, even though former US President Ronald Reagan is also said to have been a member. Bannister opened the club's first museum in 1976 and remained at the helm until current curator Fred Garbutt bought its contents in 2010.

Naturally the enthusiastic Fred wears all yellow and drives a banana-coloured Volkswagen Beetle. Banana memorabilia covers every inch of the museum space, and at the end of your visit – half an hour is probably long enough to see everything – you can drop in to the Banana Bar and sip a banana milkshake or banana soda while sitting on banana-decorated stools. Visitors can also have their photos taken wearing banana costumes.

The museum will never change under Fred's watch. 'It's going to stay family-friendly,' he says. 'It's a banana museum, there's no reason to put anything in there that you wouldn't want your children to see. I'm sure there are a lot of battery-operated objects that would not be appropriate.'

ADDRESS: 98775 CA-111, Mecca, CA 92254, USA

TEL: +1 619 840 1429

EMAIL: ibmbigbanana@aol.com

WEBSITE: www.internationalbananamuseum.com

OPEN: Officially Monday–Friday, 10 a.m.–6 p.m., but visitors are advised to phone first as opening hours may vary.

ADMISSION: $1, but free if you buy something inside.

TRASH MUSEUM, HARTFORD, CONNECTICUT

If one man's trash is another man's treasure, this place is a veritable gold mine. Covering an area of 6,500 square feet, the museum, which opened in 1992 at an operational recycling plant, hosts educational exhibits about landfills, waste management, composting and the process of converting trash into energy. In short, it lifts the lid off garbage.

A mural depicts the history of trash management from prehistoric times to today, revealing, among other things, that the refuse collectors of nineteenth-century America were often pigs that ran wild in city streets, eating everyone's trash. And they didn't expect a tip at Christmas. Another exhibit is devoted to the work of David Chameides, or Sustainable Dave as he became known, a Los Angeles native who recycled just about everything for an entire year. Whereas the average American produces around 2,000 pounds of trash annually, Sustainable Dave's final tally came in at a mere 27.5 pounds, making him the biggest green hero since The Incredible Hulk.

The museum is aimed largely at schoolchildren, for whom activities include a scavenger hunt among a vast sculpture of reclaimed garbage called the Temple of Trash. Kids also have the opportunity to build craft items out of objects that would normally be thrown away. This must be great news for their mothers, who will now never be able to get rid of old toilet rolls and bottle tops without them first being turned into a space rocket.

The highlight for many visitors will be the viewing platform from where you can watch workers sorting through piles of rubbish – part of the 300 tons of waste that the system processes every day. The viewing experience is enhanced by the presence of sixteen closed-circuit cameras, which means you need never miss a moment of the action anywhere on the site. It may not sound especially riveting, but TV reality series have been based on flimsier ideas.

The gift shop has a wide range of trash-related items for sale. Alas, a calendar showing Great Landfill Sites of the World is not among them.

ADDRESS:	211 Murphy Road, Hartford, CT 06114, USA
TEL:	+1 860 757 7765
EMAIL:	education@ctmira.org
WEBSITE:	www.ctmira.org
OPEN:	September–June, Wednesday–Friday, noon–4p.m.; July–August, Tuesday–Friday, 10 a.m.–4 p.m. Closed holidays.
ADMISSION:	$4 adults and children over 2 years.

LUNCH BOX MUSEUM, COLUMBUS, GEORGIA

When Allen Woodall declares that his Georgia emporium is home to the largest lunch box museum in the world, few are going to argue with him. After all, his collection consists of around 3,500 metal lunch boxes and their matching Thermos flasks, mostly decorated in the designs of popular childhood icons of the day, ranging from Flipper to Hopalong Cassidy and Scooby Doo to, er, Charlie's Angels. What he doesn't know about metal lunch boxes isn't worth knowing, as befits the author of the seminal tome *The Illustrated Encyclopedia of Metal Lunch Boxes*, published in 1992 and revised in 1999.

Metal lunch boxes made their bow in 1920s America, but the first models usually had plain lids or simple drawings of trains, until Disney saw the promotional benefits of placing images of their characters on children's merchandise. The advent of television in the 1950s resulted in a boom period for lunch box design. The picture on your lunch box could speak volumes about your character. A boy with a Rambo lunch box was less likely to be picked on than one whose banana sandwich and Kit-Kat were encased in an image of the Osmonds. Unfortunately the metal boxes themselves were often being used as skull-smashing truncheons in American school playground fights – a situation that led a group of Florida mothers to campaign for their abolition. Florida's stance saw other states follow suit, and the last metal lunch box was produced in 1985. As production switched to skull-friendlier vinyl, the old illegal metal boxes suddenly became collectible. Allen Woodall's passion for the colourful boxes had first manifested itself in the purchase of The Green Hornet and Dick Tracy boxes at a flea market as a child in the 1940s, and when in 1989 he acquired the late Bob Carr's collection of 750 lunch boxes, he promised Carr's widow that he would keep collecting and put them all in a museum. Twelve years later, he did just that.

Arranged in alphabetical order several tiers high, the boxes line all four walls of the museum's large room and cover the whole gamut of modern American pop culture: Batman, Superman, Planet of the Apes, Gentle Ben, the Bee Gees, Teddy Ruxpin, Zorro, the Harlem Globetrotters, the Bionic Woman, the A-Team, Yoda – they're all here. Among the rarer items, some of which are worth up to $10,000, is a 1930s electric lunch box designed to keep your meal warm.

'When a lot of people come, they have in mind the box that they had in school,' says Allen. 'They start looking for that box, and, boy, when they see it, I see that smile on their face.' In case you're wondering, Allen used to carry his lunch to school in a boring brown paper bag.

ADDRESS: River Market Antiques and Art Center, 318 10th Avenue, Columbus, GA 31901, USA

TEL: +1 706 653 6240

OPEN: Wednesday–Friday, 10 a.m.–5 p.m.; Saturday, Sunday, 9 a.m.–5 p.m. Weekday times may vary, so call in advance.

ADMISSION: $6 adults; $3 children.

HOBO MUSEUM, BRITT, IOWA

You could be forgiven for thinking there's not much to celebrate in the life of a hobo – drifting from town to town, enduring poverty, often sleeping rough – but this museum shows that there's a lot more to the average hobo than a straggly beard, a bottle of white cider and a dog on a string.

According to the accepted definition, 'a hobo wanders and works, a tramp wanders and dreams, and a bum neither wanders nor works.' Whether this alternative lifestyle is chosen or forced upon them through circumstance varies from person to person, but every year on the second weekend of August the town of Britt, Iowa, holds a Hobo Convention, attended by hundreds of itinerant workers from right across the United States, plus local people who dress down for the occasion. It features marching bands, flea markets, a 10K hobo walk and the all-important coronation of the King and Queen of the Hobos.

The idea for a Hobo Museum dates back to the 1980s with a simple box of artefacts, but became a reality when an old cinema in Britt was bought by the Hobo Foundation with money bequeathed in the will of a hobo benefactor known as Slow Motion Shorty. The display includes poems, artworks, books and music by hobos from all over the world, as well as hobo walking sticks, battered jackets, a collection of old hobo dolls and a mock-up of a hobo fire pit. Photographs, postcards, personal journals and videos describe the hobo's train-hopping existence alongside the memorabilia of famous old hobos such as Scoopshovel Scottie (revered for his tasty stew), Frisco Jack and Connecticut Slim. The last-named, who died in 1990, is brought back to life by way of a department store mannequin dressed in clothes so neatly ironed it looks as though he had been travelling first class rather than hitching an illegal ride on a freight train. If you want to show your support for hobos without the hassle of living rough, T-shirts, caps and other souvenirs are available at the gift shop.

ADDRESS:	51 Main Avenue South, Britt, IA 50423, USA
TEL:	+1 641 843 9104
OPEN:	June–August, Monday–Friday, 10 a.m.–5 p.m. Other times of the year by appointment.
ADMISSION:	$2

KANSAS BARBED WIRE MUSEUM, LA CROSSE, KANSAS

New York is often promoted as 'The City That Never Sleeps', Rome has always been 'The Eternal City' and Bruges likes to call itself the 'Venice of the North'. Well, the town of La Crosse, Kansas (population 1,342), is equally proud to be known as 'The Barbed Wire Capital of the World'. Every year during the first weekend in May, barbed wire collectors (a surprisingly numerous breed) from all over the United States descend on La Crosse for a festival dedicated solely to barbed wire, the highlight of which for many is the World Barbed Wire Splicing Contest. Fence fixing has never been so tough.

More than the six-gun or even John Wayne, barbed wire has widely been credited with single-handedly taming the Wild West, enabling ranchers to fence in their livestock and keep unwelcome intruders at bay. If it were not for barbed wire, cattle would probably be roaming Sunset Boulevard or Miami Beach in their thousands. It was invented in 1874 by Joseph Glidden, whose wife Lucinda simply wanted their garden fenced off, and quickly flourished into a multi-million-dollar industry under the slogan 'Cheaper than dirt and stronger than steel'.

To the uninitiated, all barbed wire (or as Native Americans cursed it, 'the devil's rope') looks pretty much the same, but the Kansas Barbed Wire Museum is home to more than 2,400 varieties, mostly collected by one Gary Spilger during a lifetime of selfless dedication, although some of the differences are so subtle as to be almost undetectable to any eye other than that of a true connoisseur. The museum originally opened in 1970 by popular demand from the Kansas Barbed Wire Collectors Association, and proved such a draw that in 1990 it moved to larger premises. Today it chronicles the history of the product, notably its role in both World Wars, while visitors can also watch it being made on a replica of Glidden's equipment. Exhibits include a genuine raven's nest built primarily of barbed wire and retrieved from a tree in the 1960s. There is also a range of antique fencing tools, a selection of old liniment bottles and ointment tins that promised to heal wounds caused to man or beast by barbed wire, and even a Barbed Wire Hall of Fame.

Unless you are a real devotee, an hour around the museum should be plenty long enough to satisfy your curiosity, but by the end you might find that you, too, are hooked on barbed wire.

ADDRESS:	120 West 1st Street, La Crosse, KS 67548, USA
TEL:	+1 785 222 9900
WEBSITE:	www.rushcounty.org/barbedwiremuseum
OPEN:	1 May–31 August, Monday–Saturday, 10 a.m.–4.30 p.m.; Sunday, 1 p.m.–4.30 p.m.
ADMISSION:	Free (donations welcome)

VENT HAVEN MUSEUM, FORT MITCHELL, KENTUCKY

Depending on your feelings about ventriloquists' dummies, this will either be one of the most interesting show business museums you are ever likely to visit, or the spookiest. The world's only ventriloquism museum, Vent Haven is home to around 800 dummies dating back as far as the late nineteenth century, some with human hair and real teeth. Surrounded by so many of them in a room and looking at their staring eyes, it is hard not to think Chucky.

Yet the dummies at Vent Haven, once perched on the knees of master ventriloquists like Edgar Bergen, were designed to entertain people, not freak them out. The majority of the exhibits were acquired by businessman and amateur ventriloquist William Shakespeare Berger, and following his death his private collection was turned into a public museum, Vent Haven, which opened in 1974.

The more refined dummies have a full range of facial expressions, with ears that wiggle, eyebrows that move, tongues that stick out, eyes that cross and alarming fright wigs. There are life-sized dummies, dummies that walk and even one that converts into a grandfather clock. There are dummies of former US Presidents Jimmy Carter and Ronald Reagan, both of which appear markedly less wooden than their human counterparts. There is also apparently a Hitler dummy but, rather like the Hitler Pez dispenser at the Burlingame museum, it is kept in storage and never put on display. Perhaps the most sinister are the four dummies who were the only survivors of a 1908 shipwreck in the Gulf of Mexico. Leading American ventriloquist Will Wood and his daughter died in the incident, but his dolls Woo Woo, Clown, Mary Lou and Mike were washed ashore in a trunk. After Wood's widow said she wanted nothing to do with them, probably considering them to be bad omens, they ended up at Vent Haven, which is essentially a retirement home for dummies.

As the good people at Vent Haven point out, dummies are not actually as scary as clowns and, technically, Chucky is a doll, not a dummy. So there. Even so, dummies can still get you into trouble. When Mae West told Edgar Bergen's famous sidekick Charlie McCarthy, 'I remember our date and have the splinters to prove it,' she was banned from NBC airwaves for the next twelve years.

The problem is that some people read too much into dummies. You just have to remember that they're not flesh and blood, they're made of wood. They are not real people – because real people can talk even when the person next to them is drinking a glass of water.

ADDRESS:	33 West Maple Avenue, Fort Mitchell, KY 41011, USA
TEL:	+1 859 341 0461
EMAIL:	curator@venthavenmuseum.com
WEBSITE:	venthavenmuseum.com
OPEN:	May–September. All tours are guided and by appointment.
ADMISSION:	Donation $10 per person; $5, seniors, children 12 and under, and groups of 10 or more.

UMBRELLA COVER MUSEUM, PEAKS ISLAND, MAINE

Back in 1992, eccentric Peaks Island musician Nancy 3. Hoffman discovered half a dozen umbrella covers lying in her closet with nothing to cover. She found herself inspired by the empty sheaths, realising that they are one of the few items that people rarely use but don't throw away either. Instead, they just accumulate at the bottom of cupboards every time a new umbrella is bought. Sensing that she was on to something big, she set about acquiring more covers from friends and family, and when her collection had reached around 35, she presided over a formal ribbon-cutting ceremony in 1996, and officially opened the world's only umbrella cover museum in the kitchen of her home.

With an enthusiasm fired by the knowledge that her collection is truly unique, Hoffman has gone on to acquire more than 1,300 different covers from over sixty countries, forcing her to move the museum out of the kitchen in 2000 to slightly larger, two-room premises elsewhere on the island near the ferry landing. In a vast variety of colours and fabrics (including velvet, silk, wool, porcelain, leather, rubber, duct tape, bubble gum wrappers and bulletproof Kevlar), they hang from walls and ceilings or are neatly set out on shelves and in display cases. They range in size from a tiny two-and-a-half-inch-long Barbie doll accessory to a six-foot patio umbrella sleeve. Each cover is accompanied by its provenance and back story. One simple black cover was found in 2007 next to a still-standing section of the Berlin Wall, apparently discarded by a couple during a romantic moment. A Peaks Island native who now lives in the German city happened to be cycling by at the time and picked it up for the museum. The museum states that its mission is 'dedicated to the appreciation of the mundane in everyday life. It is about finding wonder and beauty in the simplest of things, and about knowing that there is always a story behind the cover.'

In a smaller room adjoining the main attraction, Hoffman houses a display of 'sexy' umbrella covers, chiefly animal prints such as leopardskin. Addressing the more salacious side of her collection, she concedes: 'I am aware of the phallic nature of umbrella covers. I can't deny it. It wasn't foremost in my mind when I started the museum.'

When asked why she legally changed her middle name from Arlene to a number, Hoffman replies, 'Because I always wanted to.' For someone who has spent the last three decades of her life collecting umbrella covers that seems as good an explanation as any.

Peaks Island is accessible from mainland Portland by a twenty-minute journey on the Casco Bay Lines ferry, the oldest ferry service in the United States. The museum is only open in the summer months before Hoffman migrates south for winter. She usually conducts the tours herself, often while playing 'Let a Smile Be Your Umbrella' on the accordion. Her quirky museum will put a smile on your face on the rainiest of days.

ADDRESS: 62-B Island Avenue, Peaks Island, ME 04108, USA

TEL: +1 207 939 0301

EMAIL: info@umbrellacovermuseum.org

WEBSITE: www.umbrellacovermuseum.org

OPEN: Summer, Tuesday–Saturday, 10 a.m.–1 p.m.,

2 p.m.–5 p.m.; Sunday, 10 a.m.–12.30 p.m. Email or call to confirm opening times before making the trip.

ADMISSION: A $2 donation is requested.

NATIONAL MUSEUM OF DENTISTRY, BALTIMORE, MARYLAND

A trip to the dentist is nobody's idea of a fun day out, but a trip to the National Museum of Dentistry is an altogether more pleasurable experience. Not only do you get to look at some of the great molars in history and the fearsome equipment that was used to treat them, but nobody is going to drill into your teeth, prod your fillings with a sharp metal hook or force you to read issues of *Country Life* or *Woman's Weekly* from 2004.

The Dr Samuel D. Harris Museum of National Dentistry opened wide in 1996 on the campus of the University of Maryland, which in 1840 was the home of the world's first dental school. You soon realise that you will be required to grit your teeth throughout the tour when you come across exhibits marked 'Development of Drills' and 'Evolution of Extraction Instruments', featuring weapons dating back to the eighteenth century with names like 'The Key'. This device had a hinged 'claw' that grasped the tooth, which was then pulled by turning it like a key ... years before painkillers or anaesthetics became commonplace. Displays also recall the good old days when urine was used as a mouthwash – a fact many find hard to swallow.

Highlights of the 40,000-strong collection include George Washington's dentures, which were not made of wood as legend had it but from the real teeth of hippos, cows and people. Elsewhere, an assortment of malevolent dental instruments that were used on Queen Victoria makes it little surprise that she was never amused. When you've had enough of looking at teeth, you can study a range of novelty toothbrushes featuring the likes of Mickey Mouse and Fred Flintstone, or the 'Toothbrushes Through the Ages' exhibit, from its ancient Egyptian 'chew stick' – in essence a twig with a frayed end – right up to today's hi-tech electric brushes. There is also the chance to sing along to a selection of old TV toothpaste commercials on the world's only jukebox dedicated to teeth. Yes, you'll wonder where the yellow went when you brush your teeth with Pepsodent.

If you want to go back to the roots of dentistry, you will not be disappointed by your visit. It's easy enough to find, although you'd think a dental museum would have a little plaque on the wall.

ADDRESS: 31 South Greene Street, Baltimore, MD 21201, USA

TEL: +1 410 706 0600

WEBSITE: www.dental.umaryland.edu

OPEN: By appointment.

ADMISSION: $7 adults, $6 seniors and students, $5 children 3–12 years.

BURNT FOOD MUSEUM, ARLINGTON, MASSACHUSETTS

This private museum was founded accidentally in 1989, when professional harpist but amateur cook Deborah Henson-Conant put on a small pot of hot apple cider to heat, only to be interrupted by a very long phone call. By the time she returned to the kitchen, her cider had become a 'cinder'. 'When the curtain of thick black smoke finally cleared in the kitchen,' she recalls, 'I discovered this amazing gem, the free-standing hot apple cider, inside the completely blackened pot. Thus began my fascination with the beauty of burnt food. People think burnt food is a negative thing, but it's really important, before you claim failure, to stop and take a look at what you've done and find the beauty in it.'

The cremated remains of that dish were so strangely impressive she decided to keep them, adding more of her culinary disasters along the way, including a 'thrice baked potato', a lemon that spontaneously combusted and an unfortunate quiche. Once she left sweet potatoes in the oven when she headed off to Mexico, and returned five weeks later to 'a fossilised mess that had been slow cooked by the pilot light.'

As founder, curator and prime contributor to the museum, Henson-Conant clearly belongs to the school of cooks who use a smoke alarm as a timer. She is always looking to add exhibits, and welcomes burnt offerings from other inept, easily-distracted or just plain unlucky cooks. Their enthusiasm for 'Food Noir' has encouraged them to submit for exhibition such mishaps as a chicken that appears to have been barbecued for several months, a torched muffin, an RIP pizza, something that in safer hands could have been lasagne, some truly spectacular hash blacks, and more charred toast than you can shake a fire extinguisher at. She does stipulate that all submissions must be accidental, not deliberate, because for her the story behind the burning is as important as the item itself. As an example she relates the tale of a pregnant woman who basted a turkey for Thanksgiving and promptly went into premature labour. Six days later, she came home to something that was essentially a turkey shell.

The museum's exhibits are largely kept in storage at Henson-Conant's house, but she can occasionally provide personal guided tours by prior appointment only. Alternatively, many of the crispy specimens may be viewed online at the website www.burntfood-museum.com. As with any self-respecting museum, there is an online gift shop selling aprons, T-shirts and mugs, but no cookery books. The museum also has its own motto: 'To cook the Burnt Food Museum way, always leave the flame on low . . . and then take a long nap.'

CONTACT:	Twitter @BurntFoodMuseum or via the BurntFoodMuseum Facebook page
EMAIL:	info@hipharp.com
WEBSITE:	www.burntfoodmuseum.com
OPEN:	By prior appointment with curator.

MUSEUM OF BAD ART, SOMERVILLE, MASSACHUSETTS

In 1994, antique dealer Scott Wilson discovered a painting lying among a pile of garbage waiting to be collected at the roadside in Boston, Massachusetts. He was initially only interested in the frame, but his friend Jerry Reilly thought the picture, *Lucy in the Field with Flowers*, was so bad it was almost good. Reilly exhibited the painting in his home and encouraged friends to hunt out other examples of bad art. As the collection grew, Reilly and his wife, Marie Jackson, held a reception at their home titled 'The Opening of the Museum of Bad Art'. 'While every city in the world has at least one museum dedicated to the best of art,' explained Reilly, 'MOBA is the only museum dedicated to collecting and exhibiting the worst.'

To warrant consideration by MOBA, a painting needed to have serious intent but be flawed. Anything that was deliberately painted to look awful or was the work of a child was rejected. As Jackson said, 'We are here to celebrate an artist's right to fail, gloriously.'

At first, MOBA created a Virtual Museum of Bad Art, an imaginary exhibition on a CD-ROM, but when a bus load of soon-to-be disappointed senior citizens turned up one day hoping to see a real museum, the curators decided to seek out a tangible setting and found one in the basement of the Dedham Community Centre, appropriately just outside the toilets. Very much the *Mona Lisa* of the collection was R. Angelo Le's portrait *Eileen*, another painting Wilson had rescued from a tip, and which had been slashed with a knife even before the museum acquired it, thereby 'adding an additional element of drama to an already powerful work.' When *Eileen* was stolen in 1996, MOBA offered a generous – some might say, reckless – reward of $6.50 for its return. Stung

217

into action, the museum installed a fake video camera on the premises with a sign reading, 'Warning. This gallery is protected by a fake security camera.'

Living down to its motto 'Art too bad to be ignored', the museum offers such gems as *Sunday on the Pot with George*, a picture by an unknown artist of a portly man in Y-fronts sitting on a chamber pot, *Mana Lisa*, a cross-gender interpretation of the da Vinci classic, and Mari Newman's *Juggling Dog in Hula Skirt*. Newman, a professional artist, revealed that she painted it in her student days as a failed experiment. 'I almost threw it out until I heard of MOBA, 'she wrote. 'After many years of slashing rejected work, now I wish I had saved them all for you.'

These days MOBA has three small galleries in the Boston area. Of over 600 pieces in the permanent collection, there is only room to exhibit around thirty at a time at each location. If you're lucky you might spot the painting that started it all, *Lucy in the Field with Flowers*, a work hailed by Kate Swoger of the *Montreal Gazette* as 'a glorious mistake'. She went on to describe Lucy as 'An elderly woman dancing in a lush spring field, sagging breasts flopping willy-nilly, as she inexplicably seems to hold a red chair to her behind with one hand and a clutch of daisies in the other.' Author Cash Peters summarised the unintentional masterpiece succinctly as 'the old woman with an armchair glued to her ass.' Some years later, Boston-area nurse Susan Lawlor saw the portrait in a newspaper and recognised it as being of her late grand-mother, Anna Lally Keane. It had been commissioned by Lawlor's mother, who apparently was quite pleased with the result, and the painting had hung in Lawlor's aunt's living room for many years before being thrown out following a house clearance. 'The face is hauntingly hers,' Lawlor admitted, 'but everything else is so horribly wrong.'

ADDRESS: Somerville Theatre, 55 Davis Square, Somerville,
MA 02144, USA

TEL: +1 781 444 6757

EMAIL: Info@MuseumOfBadArt.org

WEBSITE: www.museumofbadart.org

OPEN: Whenever films are showing at the Somerville
Theatre.

ADMISSION: Free with the purchase of an admission ticket to
an event at the theatre.

MOBA currently exhibits at two other Massachusetts locations: the New England Wildlife Center, 500 Columbian St., South Weymouth, MA 02190, open Monday, Wednesday, Thursday, Friday, 10 a.m.–4 p.m.; Tuesday, 10 a.m.–7 p.m.; Saturday, 10 a.m. –9 p.m.; Sunday, 10 a.m.–2 p.m.; and in the offices of the Brookline Interactive Group, 46 Tappan St., Brookline, MA 02445, open Monday–Thursday, 8 a.m.–8 p.m.; Friday, 10 a.m.–4 p.m. Admission to both galleries is free.

MOIST TOWELETTE MUSEUM, EAST LANSING, MICHIGAN

Whereas at the Louvre or the Natural History Museum you sometimes have to battle your way through crowds, there are no such problems at the Moist Towelette Museum. For this joyous but compact display is located in the collector's office at Michigan State University, where it attracts only occasional visitors, although someone did once drive all the way from Chicago. Suffice to say that in most years Captain Hook could count the total visitor numbers on his bad hand.

John French, production co-ordinator at the Abrams Planetarium, began collecting moist towelettes (or wet wipes) around twenty years ago for reasons that elude him to this day. When pressed on the matter, he suspects that it coincided with the birth of strange internet collections, and he spotted a gap in the market with moist towelettes. He now has around 1,000, most of them spread in unopened packets over eight small bookshelves in his office. The oldest dates back to 1963, and he also has specimens from the Hard Rock Café in Beijing, Planet Hollywood in London, a Turkish petrol station, a sumo wrestling match in Japan, Lufthansa Airlines, British Airways, Russian Railways and the US Embassy in Sweden. One of the more unusual is the Radiacwash, designed to wipe away radioactive contamination. Others have been made specifically for cleaning musical instruments, dentures and the pinky fingers of secretaries.

Many of these have been received via donations or by swapping with other moist towelette collectors – and, yes, there are some. 'I wish I had been to all the places these moist towelettes have been,' says John. 'I'm not nearly as travelled as they are.'

Although he has a pack of *Star Trek* towelettes from the series's original run (bearing images of Kirk and Spock), he has resisted the temptation to ask celebrities for theirs. 'I thought that might be a little weird,' he admits. Indeed, the only item in what he calls the 'celebrity wing' of the museum is a used (and therefore no longer moist) towelette donated by Tom and Ray Magliozzi, hosts of US radio show *Car Talk*. Even so, he doesn't rule out approaching Miley Cyrus for a moist towelette some time in the future.

Of course, the small number of visitors to the museum is no reflection of the worldwide interest in moist towelettes – it's simply that most enthusiasts prefer to visit the online exhibition. If they all turned up at John French's office he would never get any work done, although he stresses that if anyone happens to be in the area and wants to pop in for a few minutes, he will be happy to show them around one of the world's weirdest museums and talk towelettes (moist).

ADDRESS:	Room 100, Abrams Planetarium, Michigan State University, 755 Science Road, East Lansing, MI 48824, USA
TEL:	+1 517 355 4676
WEBSITE:	moisttowelettemuseum.com
OPEN:	Tuesday–Friday, 9.30 a.m.–4.30 p.m.
ADMISSION:	Free

INTERNATIONAL UFO MUSEUM AND RESEARCH CENTER, ROSWELL, NEW MEXICO

In July 1947, something occurred during a severe thunderstorm 75 miles north-west of Roswell, New Mexico. The first press release issued by Walter Haut, the public information officer at Roswell Army Air Field, sensationally announced the capture of a flying saucer. The following day, a new bulletin said it was, in fact, just a weather balloon. No spaceship, no little green men. But weather balloons make for neither conspiracy theories nor a tourist industry, and so over the course of time the Roswell Incident, as it has become known, has mushroomed into a monumental military cover-up, involving a crashed flying saucer and the secret recovery of debris and alien bodies. A mortician working at a local funeral home would reveal that in the aftermath of the incident, the RAAF mortuary officer had sent out a request for a number of small, hermetically sealed coffins. Other witnesses came forward to describe seeing strange pieces of spaceship-type metal lying on the ground, but their evidence usually generated more questions than answers. The more the US military insisted that it was nothing other than a weather balloon, the more ufologists became convinced that extraterrestrials had landed back in 1947. Roswell was now the Earth's number one alien hotspot.

To cater for the wealth of interest in the Roswell Incident, Lt Haut wanted to build a museum to educate the public about what may or may not be out there. It opened in 1992, and has since attracted hundreds of thousands of visitors from all over the world, and perhaps beyond.

Obviously the major part of the exhibition deals with what is known about the events of seventy years ago. Visitors can study a container of dirt taken from the supposed crash site, examine models of the terrain, see a reconstruction of how any aliens may have looked as they stepped onto American soil, and read about the various conflicting accounts. To add a little Hollywood gloss to proceedings, there is the dummy of an alien corpse that appeared in the 1994 movie *Roswell: The UFO Cover-up*, and the weapon used by Sigourney Weaver to fight the alien in *Aliens*. As well as reports of other UFO sightings, the museum looks at unexplained phenomena such as crop circles, and recounts startling tales of alien abduction for that essential 'Beam me up' moment. As you would expect, the gift shop is out of this world.

Non-believers probably won't find anything here to change their views, but the admission prices are modest and aliens can get in free.

ADDRESS:	114 North Main Street, Roswell, NM 88203, USA
TEL:	+1 575 625 9495
WEBSITE:	www.roswellufomuseum.com
OPEN:	Daily, 9 a.m.–5 p.m., except Thanksgiving, Christmas Day and New Year's Day.
ADMISSION:	$5, adults, $2, children 5–15 years.

ELEVATOR HISTORICAL SOCIETY MUSEUM, NEW YORK CITY

Life for Patrick Carrajat has had its ups and downs, not only because he has been divorced twice, but also because he is simply wild about elevators. His father worked as an elevator repairman, and young Patrick used to savour the days when he was allowed to help him at work. 'Like a butcher's kid learns to cut meat, I learned to fix elevators,' he says. Patrick has since taken his passion to another level. He has been collecting elevator artefacts since 1955, and in 2011 opened a museum displaying around 2,000 items linked to elevator history.

The museum is located on the second floor of a building in the Queens borough of New York and, somewhat ironically, is reached via a flight of stairs. It occupies a single room designed to look like the inside of an elevator. Paintings of elevators and escalators line the walls along with photos of elevator operators from bygone years. Mementos include dial indicators, operator uniforms and ceiling lights from different decades, an assortment of company plaques that once adorned elevators, old instruction manuals, early Otis Elevator Company order books, a set of Otis cast iron plates from the 1860s, a White House elevator inspection certificate, an elevator handbrake from 1896 and, from more recent times, a signed photo of Leonardo Di Caprio and Kate Winslet inside an elevator from the movie *Titanic*. The shelves are also stocked with elevator manufacturing merchandise such as cigarette lighters and golf balls. One of the most significant exhibits is an 1895 Otis push button, the very first call system for elevators. 'Before that,' says Patrick, 'it was just someone banging on the door if they wanted to use the elevator.'

As befits someone who once ran his own elevator company, Patrick's guided tour of the museum, which receives about 500 visitors a year, contains a wealth of elevator history, including the so-called 'elevator disease' of 1903, when elevators fell up instead of down because they were balanced incorrectly. It sounds like an April Fool's story, but Patrick is not one to joke about elevators.

If anyone should doubt his command of his chosen field, it should be noted that he has testified as an expert witness in more than 100 cases of elevator and escalator-related injury, of which there are apparently around 1,500 each year in New York alone. Unsurprisingly he is a stickler for accuracy, and has written to a number of Hollywood directors pointing out elevator-related mistakes in their movies. It takes real single-mindedness to watch a movie solely for its elevator scenes.

ADDRESS: Suite 206, 39–43 21st Street, Queens, New York, NY11101, USA

TEL: +1 917 748 2328

EMAIL: patrick@elevatorhistory.org

WEBSITE: www.elevatorhistory.org

OPEN: By appointment.

ADMISSION: Free

MMUSEUMM, NEW YORK CITY

Tucked down an alley in the Tribeca district of Manhattan lies New York's most secret and probably its strangest museum. Founded by Alex Kalman and film-maker brothers Benny and Josh Safdie in 2012, Mmuseumm has exhibited such random items as a facsimile of the shoe thrown at George W. Bush during a 2008 press conference, papers accidentally left behind in copy machines and a collection of plastic vomit from around the world. Yet it is not only the subject matter that makes this one-room space stand out from the crowd – it is the fact that it is housed in an abandoned freight elevator. Patrick Carrajat probably can't keep away. Visitors are only admitted to the elevator at certain hours (and there is not room for more than four at a time), but even when the forbidding iron shutters are closed, a series of small viewing windows allow passers-by to marvel at the wonders within whenever they happen to be in the area.

Mmuseumm – all 36 square feet of it – describes itself as 'a modern natural history museum dedicated to the curation and exhibition of contemporary artefacts that illustrate the complexities of the modern world.' The only items on permanent display are a handful of suitably eclectic objects that have been lost and found in cities across the world over the past ten years. They include a motel charge card, a hot water coil heater from Lithuania, a home-made antenna and a Saudi Arabian packet of cheese puffs. The remainder of the exhibition changes every three months, which means you may miss out on such gems as a collection of news-stand paperweights, three personal possessions found in the Pacific Ocean by Mark Cunningham (a comb, a driver's licence card and a mobile phone), an assortment of New York City tip jars, plastic coffee cup lids, a series of home-made gas masks, objects made by prison inmates, toothpaste tubes from around the world, items removed from patients' stomachs by a Massachusetts doctor, a collection of plastic spoons, misspelled food container labels and, perhaps most memorably of all, 200 dead mosquitoes. The insects were killed mid-bite in New Delhi over the course of the monsoon season and turned into a splendid collection by one Zachary Becker.

As word spread, avant-garde artists began sending their quirky creations for exhibition at Mmuseumm. English artist Anne Griffiths devotes her time and energy to categorising and classifying different sizes and shapes of corn flakes, in the same manner that nineteenth-century naturalists did with butterflies, and as such her unique board of over thirty corn flakes – each one slightly different – fitted in perfectly with the no-theme theme of Mmuseumm.

Kalman's idea for turning disused city space into a museum for largely useless items acquired over the years proved so popular that in 2015, three doors down, he opened Mmuseumm 2: twenty square feet of storefront window exhibition space in which his artist mother Maira painstakingly recreated the immaculately pressed, minimalist, all-white wardrobe of her own mother, Sara Berman. 'When she died in 2004,' says Ms Kalman, 'I just had the complete sense that her closet would be an amazing museum, and people would love to come and see it. She was an extraordinary woman, very chic, very funny and she wore only white.'

Mmuseumm expresses the hope that 'by examining the small things, we are able to look at the big one, life itself, or at least start to see its edges.' Thus a run-down, unloved, graffiti-strewn area of the city that was once used chiefly as a realistic setting for TV crime dramas, where bodies are found in alleys on a weekly basis and the crime is always solved in one hour (minus commercial breaks), has now been transformed into New York's unlikeliest museum quarter.

ADDRESS:	4 Cortlandt Alley (between Franklin Street and White Street), New York, NY 10013, USA
TEL:	+1 888 763 8839
EMAIL:	info@Mmuseumm.com
WEBSITE:	www.mmuseumm.com
OPEN:	Thursday, Friday, 6–9 p.m.; Saturday, Sunday, noon–6 p.m. Exhibits can be viewed 24/7 through the windows.
ADMISSION:	$5 donation welcomed.

KAZOO FACTORY AND MUSEUM, BEAUFORT, SOUTH CAROLINA

Two gentlemen from Macon, Georgia, Alabama Vest and Thaddeus Von Clegg, are widely credited with inventing the voice-changing instrument, the kazoo, around 1842. As a result of its shape it became known as the 'Down South Submarine', the name 'kazoo' not appearing until 1883 in a patent by Warren Herbert Frost. Meanwhile in 1852, travelling salesman Emil Sorg had stumbled across one of Vest and Von Clegg's pieces, but it took him another sixty years to put it into production with New York ironsmith Michael McIntyre. So at least five different people played key roles in the development of one of the few home-grown American musical instruments.

As such, the kazoo warrants not just one, but two museums – this establishment in South Carolina and another in Eden, New York. Home to the collection of kazoo enthusiast and TV person-ality Boaz Frankel, the Kazoo Museum first opened in 2007 in Seattle, before moving to Portland, Oregon, in 2008 and then to Beaufort, South Carolina, in 2010. It is now located in a special building at the factory of Kazoobie Kazoos, who, as every kazoo aficionado will tell you, are one of the world's largest manufactur-ers of plastic kazoos, with around 750,000 produced every year. Early kazoos were marketed as the perfect accessory for mimick-ing the sounds of Punch and Judy, birds, animals or the bagpipes. Yes, someone actually thought that recreating the sound of the bagpipes was a selling point.

Today the museum houses more than 200 kazoo-related items, including electric kazoos, novelty kazoos shaped like cartoon characters and the very kazoo that was used in an episode of *The Partridge Family*. Some of the kazoos on display are over 100 years old. Visitors can learn about the instrument's history and manufacture, from an old press that was once used to make kazoo parts to a tour of the factory to see modern production methods. At the end of the tour, you can even make your own kazoo, which is, according to Kazoobie, 'America's most beloved musical instrument'. They could just be a little biased.

ADDRESS:	12 John Galt Road, Beaufort, SC 29906, USA
TEL:	+1 843 982 6387
WEBSITE:	kazoomuseum.org
OPEN:	Monday–Friday, 9 a.m.–5 p.m.
ADMISSION:	Free (museum only); $5 (guided tour of factory and museum).

If South Carolina is too far out of your way, but you remain desperate to visit a kazoo museum, try the **Kazoo Boutique and Museum** at 8703 South Main Street, Eden, NY 14057. The phone number is +1 716 992 3960, or you can contact them via edenkazoo@gmail.com.

SALT AND PEPPER SHAKER MUSEUM, GATLINBURG, TENNESSEE

Little did Belgian-born anthropologist Andrea Ludden know when she bought a faulty pepper mill at a garage sale in the mid-1980s that it would be the start of a lifetime's collecting. As it didn't work properly, she bought a couple more. 'I used to stand them on the window ledge of my kitchen,' she says, 'and neighbours thought I was building a collection. Nothing could have been further from my mind!'

Soon she had around 14,000 shakers on shelves all over the house, prompting her husband Rolf to issue her with an ultimatum: 'You either find somewhere to put these things or it's a divorce.' So she created the Museum of Salt and Pepper Shakers, first in Cosby, Tennessee, and since 2005 in nearby Gatlinburg. Later, as the collection continued to grow, the Luddens opened a sister salt and pepper shaker museum, the *Museo de Saleros y Pimenteros*, in Guadalest, Spain. While Rolf acts as curator to the museum's collection of 1,500 pepper mills, Andrea is the undisputed shaker queen.

She currently has over 40,000 pairs of brightly-coloured shakers, divided between the two museums, including salt and pepper pots in such inventive shapes as headstones, human skulls, penguins, alligators, kangaroos, Daleks, nuns, monks, hippies, pirates, bikers, Coca-Cola cans, army binoculars, dice, telephones, chess pieces, umbrellas, toilets and human feet. For lovers of sixties music, there is a Beatles set (with John and George joined together as salt and Paul and Ringo as pepper), although mysteriously nothing to celebrate the more appropriate Four Seasons. Other historical sets commemorate the Apollo XI moon landing, and before-and-after versions of Mount St Helens made from genuine volcanic ash from the eruption.

The packed shelves hold shakers made from all manner of materials – animal horns, eggshells, glass, wood and porcelain – although it is disappointing to report that at home the Luddens use practical plastic.

Unsurprisingly given their shape, you can also get your hands on saucy shakers, ranging from the cheeky to the downright pornographic, but although Andrea has about sixty of these she prefers not to exhibit them in a family museum.

The museum tells you everything you could possibly want to know about the history of salt and pepper shakers, including the vexed question of the respective number of holes in each. Apparently it varies depending on availability, culture and health concerns. For example, in the UK and the United States, where excessive salt is considered bad for you, the salt shaker is the one with fewer holes, but in other parts of the world the salt shaker has more holes than the pepper shaker. Or sometimes they have the same number. Basically there is no rule.

Yet the burning question must be: how did a trained archaeologist and anthropologist end up as a seasoned salt and pepper shaker expert? Andrea explains that there is a definite link. 'It's often by looking at the apparently more mundane articles in ordinary life that you can build up a broad picture of a specific period,' she once told Smithsonian.com. 'There's almost nothing you can imagine that hasn't been copied as a salt and pepper shaker, and many of them reflect the designs, the colours and the preoccupations of the period.'

Many collectors would be tempted to rest on their laurels at 40,000, but the Luddens continue to scour the world for new specimens. Down in Tennessee there's still a whole lotta shakin' goin' on.

ADDRESS: 461 Brookside Village Way, Gatlinburg, TN 37738, USA

TEL: +1 865 430 5515

WEBSITE: thesaltandpeppershakermuseum.com

OPEN: Monday–Saturday, 10 a.m.–4 p.m.; Sunday, noon–4 p.m.

ADMISSION: $3 adults, children 12 years and under free. The admission fee goes towards any salt and pepper shaker purchase in the gift shop.

BARNEY SMITH'S TOILET SEAT ART MUSEUM, SAN ANTONIO, TEXAS

In the course of his life, Barney Smith has spent more hours in close proximity to toilet seats than all but the chronically incontinent. A master plumber by trade, for almost half a century he has devoted his spare time to converting toilet seats into works of art, to the extent that the garage behind his home in San Antonio, Texas, houses more than 1,150 imaginatively decorated seats, each with its own individual theme, varying from Scrabble to *Star Wars*. Even well into his nineties, he would be toiling until the early hours, unable to eat or sleep when working on a new seat.

Barney's unusual passion stemmed from his father, who was also a plumber and who loved mounting trophy heads on plaques. Barney noticed a similarity between the mounting boards and the toilet seats he encountered on a daily basis, and so began collecting used seats, which he would then either paint in swirling patterns or adorn with items as diverse as state vehicle licence plates, Pokémon cards and tap faucet handles. He has also created the ultimate 'hot seat' featuring working Zippo cigarette lighters. In 1992 he eventually opened this collection as a museum.

Every toilet seat tells a story. There is the OJ Simpson glove seat, tribute seats to Elvis, JFK and Michael Jackson, a seat embellished with a million dollars of shredded cash donated by the Federal Reserve Bank of San Antonio, a seat smeared with volcanic ash from the 1980 eruption of Mount St Helens, a seat dedicated to the fall of the Berlin Wall, and a seat featuring a chunk of wreckage from the *Challenger* space shuttle that exploded on take-off in 1986. Most impressive of all, perhaps, is the seat decorated with the porcelain flushing device of Saddam Hussein's toilet from his Iraq bunker. Apparently a former US Navy commander visited Saddam's underground lair in 2004 and brought back a section of the former dictator's toilet just for Barney.

Other seats are more personal. When Barney's wife underwent gallstone surgery, he decided to keep her hospital fluid bags and intravenous tubes and stick them to a toilet seat. One of the more recent seats he created was to mark his and his wife's 74th wedding anniversary shortly before her passing.

To visit the museum, you need to telephone Barney in advance and he will happily show you around. If you bring him a toilet seat, he will engrave your name on the back when it is finished. He turned 94 in 2015, but his artistic toilet seats will remain in safe hands even after his death. The Bemis Company, a leading toilet seat manufacturer, has said it would like to display Barney's unique contribution to history and popular culture at its head-quarters in Wisconsin, thus making it a true seat of learning.

ADDRESS:	239 Abiso Avenue, San Antonio, TX 78209, USA
TEL:	+1 210 824 7791
OPEN:	By appointment only.
ADMISSION:	Free, but will accept donations, especially in the form of toilet seats.

NATIONAL MUSEUM OF FUNERAL HISTORY, HOUSTON, TEXAS

A trip to the National Museum of Funeral History might seem an unlikely destination for a family day out, but each year it attracts thousands of visitors apparently eager to view its collection of coffins and vintage hearses, and to learn about the deathly rituals of various civilisations. It makes funeral history come alive.

The museum opened in 1992 to fulfil undertaker Robert L. Waltrip's dream of preserving funereal artefacts that would otherwise be discarded. There are thirteen permanent exhibits, including Japanese funerals, a display of fantasy coffins from Ghana, a history of embalming, Victorian mourning customs, and artefacts from US Presidential funerals. Among these are the original eternal flame from JFK's grave, the hearse that carried the bodies of Ronald Reagan and Gerald Ford, a lock of Abraham Lincoln's hair and the actual bill from George Washington's funeral (don't worry, it has been paid).

The one that most visitors flock to see (the equivalent of the elephant enclosure at a zoo) is the papal funeral. Created in collaboration with the Vatican, the huge exhibit features the very Popemobile used by John Paul II in 1982, a faithful reproduction of his coffin, original uniforms worn by the Swiss Guard, who are responsible for the Pope's personal security, and vestments from Gammarelli's, the tailor's shop in Rome which clothes the pontiff. The museum claims that the end result provides visitors 'with a true sense of attending a Pope's funeral' ... but in Texas, and without a real Pope, or a real death.

The least successful vehicle on show is the 1916 Packard funeral bus. Designed to carry a coffin, pallbearers and up to twenty mourners, it was climbing a steep hill in San Francisco in the

1920s when the weight of all the people in the back caused it to tip up, sending both the living and the dead rolling back down the hill. After that, it was swiftly withdrawn from service. Even more bizarre is a coffin built for three. It was made for a Colorado couple in the 1930s after their baby had tragically died. Grief-stricken, they planned to commit suicide and be buried together as a family in a single coffin, but then changed their minds, leaving the coffin unused. There is also an 1862 ventilating coffin, specially designed for rotting corpses. Naturally the museum has a gift shop, where you can purchase a mug bearing the museum's motto, 'Any day above ground is a good one', or a necklace decorated with coffin charms, the gift that says everything about the state of your relationship.

If you feel your life will be enriched by viewing the actual hearse used in Princess Grace of Monaco's funeral, or the original marble slab from Marilyn Monroe's tomb (it eventually had to be replaced because visitors wore it out by touching and kissing it), you will find plenty here to satisfy your needs. One piece of advice: should you be planning to take your parents on a trip to this museum, best not make it a surprise.

ADDRESS: 415 Barren Springs Drive, Houston, TX 77090, USA

TEL: +1 281 876 3063

EMAIL: contact@nmfh.org

WEBSITE: nmfh.org

OPEN: Monday–Friday, 10 a.m.–4 p.m.; Saturday, 10 a.m.–5 p.m.; Sunday, noon–5 p.m.

ADMISSION: $10 adults; $7 children 6–11 years.